SHONA, LUNCH GIRLS, THE SHELTER

The 1983 Verity Bargate Award-winning Sh

Chosen as outstanding by seven judges, inclu   narlotte
Cornwell and *Times* critic Irving Wardle, out   med
scripts, these three short plays were joint win   ard,
established to encourage new writers.

Shona is a moving and deeply sympathetic case history of a schizophrenic girl, the man who tries to help her and the doctor in charge of her treatment. *Lunch Girls* portrays the interweaving lives of four women in a brilliantly sustained sequence of often hilarious monologues. *The Shelter* is set in the East End during the Blitz and reveals the humour, the anxiety and the misplaced optimism of the families for whom long and frequent retreats into the bomb-shelter have become a way of life.

SHONA

by

TONY CRAZE

LUNCH GIRLS

by

RON HART

THE SHELTER

by

JOHNNIE QUARRELL

A Methuen New Theatrescript
Methuen London

A METHUEN PAPERBACK

First published as a paperback original in 1983 by Methuen London Ltd,
11 New Fetter Lane, London EC4P 4EE
Shona copyright © 1983 by Tony Craze
Lunch Girls copyright © 1983 by Ron Hart
The Shelter copyright © 1983 by Johnnie Quarrell

ISBN 0 413 53850 8

CAUTION
All rights in these plays are reserved. Applications for permission to perform them
in whole or in part must be made in advance, before rehearsals begin, to the addresses
given below.
Shona: Tony Craze c/o Methuen London Ltd.
Lunch Girls: Ron Hart c/o Methuen London Ltd.
The Shelter: Actac Ltd., 16 Cadogan Lane, London SW1.

Set in IBM 10 point Press Roman by 𝄽 Tek-Art, Croydon, Surrey
Printed in Great Britain by
Richard Clay (The Chaucer Press) Ltd, Bungay, Suffolk.

The Verity Bargate Award

In 1969 Verity Bargate and Fred Proud set up the Soho Theatre Company in Soho. It moved to its present location in Riding House Street in 1971 where it became the Soho Poly Theatre. From this base Verity gave the first helping hand to hundreds of new writers by premiering their work. She gained the theatre an international reputation for her work with new and developing writers and the one act play. Some of the writers whose early work she premiered were: Barrie Keeffe, Howard Brenton, Pam Gems, Gilly Fraser and Brian Clarke.
This award has been established to commemorate the remarkable contribution made by a woman of extraordinary instinct and drive in the field of new writing, and to carry on her work by the continuing encouragement of new playwrights.

Eligibility
The only restrictions on entries were that they should be new, unperformed short act plays and that they should be suitable for production at a small theatre such as the Soho Poly, where the winning play will be produced. The award also comprises a cash prize and publication by Methuen London Ltd.

Selection
The members of the Verity Bargate Award Committee and the Fund Raising Committee gathered to read all the entries — almost 200 — and, in consultation, drew up a shortlist of nineteen plays, from which the judges made the final selection. All plays were given the same consideration regardless of style, content and form; quality and potential were the only guidelines.

Judges
The judges for the 1983 award were: Liz Calder, of Jonathon Cape Ltd; Charlotte Cornwell, actress; Nicholas Hern, of Methuen London Ltd; Barrie Keeffe, playwright; Tony Marchant, playwright; Ann Mitchell, actress; Irving Wardle, drama critic of *The Times*. They selected the three plays printed in this volume, recommending that *Shona* should be the play given a production at the Soho Poly but that all three authors should share the cash prize and all three plays should be published.

Contents

SHONA

Characters

SHONA
HARRY
DR IAN WALL
SPEAKER'S VOICE
MEMBER'S VOICE
1ST MAN'S VOICE
2ND MAN'S VOICE
WOMAN'S VOICE

At the time of going to press, *Shona* was scheduled for production at the Soho Poly Theatre in October 1983.

This is the script as it was before rehearsals began, and it is not necessarily the script of the play as performed.

Scene One

Fade up parliamentary hubbub on radio.
SPEAKER'S VOICE: Order, order, order . . .

As MEMBER's VOICE *comes in, light* DOCTOR IAN WALL *seated at home in winged chair, dictating a lecture for transcription into a microrecorder. He works from papers placed, together with bottle and glass of red wine, on a wine table to the side of the chair. He pauses now, to listen to the* MEMBER's VOICE.

MEMBER'S VOICE: Will the Secretary of State for Social Services list in the official report, how many ECT and psychosurgery operations took place on compulsory and voluntary patients, respectively, in NHS hospitals, in each of the years between 1975 and 1981?

SECRETARY'S VOICE: Information on the number of ECT treatments is not collected centrally.

Murmurs from the bench.
The hospital inpatient enquiry records, record about 300 leucotomy, lobotomy and tractotomy operations carried out annually. But as these records are based on a one in ten sample of all non-psychiatric discharges and deaths, it will not count any operations performed within a psychiatric unit. Information is not available as to whether these operations were performed on compulsory or voluntary patients, nor whether they were performed compulsorily or voluntarily. I am considering the case for collecting more precise information on psychosurgery operations.

Hubbub increases as the DOCTOR *frowns, sips wine.*
SPEAKER'S VOICE: Order. Order.

Scene Two

SHONA, *just arrived, stands between two carrier bags, in an almost empty, bare room in a squat.* HARRY, *having shown her the room, perhaps lights a single old fashioned gas burner, puts on a kettle.*

SHONA: They said I had too much luggage down the Waterloo Road: that's why they couldn't have me they said. Before that it was another hostel up at Kings Cross. Short stay — two weeks and they throw you out. This'll be all right. It was right wasn't it, what you said — I could have it from now?

HARRY: It's all yours. The decisions are all taken together here. You got the vote.

SHONA: Never had a place that was mine. I was sharing before — before the hostel at Kings Cross. Living-in at this hotel. I lost that though, the job. No reason. I think he preferred my room-mate, the man that ran it. Where's your room?

HARRY: Downstairs. The front room.

SHONA *begins taking one or two things from her carriers, dots them about, including a picture of the Pope, which she stands somewhere.*

SHONA: I like this being small. Could have friends round. Well, could if they'd let them come. Do you think they would — just for an afternoon — if they knew they had somewhere to go?

HARRY: Would they? Bit unlikely isn't it.

SHONA: You don't have to be mad to be in hospital you know.

HARRY: Oh no — bet it helps though.

SHONA: Think I'm fucking mad then do you?

HARRY: I meant putting up with it all — shrinks. Wouldn't have let you out would they if you were?

SHONA: Oh, fuck off. I'm not mad and wasn't before.

HARRY: Sorry.

Pause.

SHONA: Don't know if I want to stay here.

HARRY: I think you should. Stay.

SHONA: Might be catching for you.

HARRY: I might already have it.

SHONA: They said it would be like this they did. People would put the old nose in the air. 'Bit fucking potty are you then?' It's not my fault they stole twelve years off my life is it?

HARRY: But you don't just get banged up in those places do you?

SHONA: How much you know. I was sent to a remand home in the beginning. I was fifteen, coming up for my sixteenth birthday when they put me under this care and protection order. But then they sent me to the remand home because they said they didn't have anywhere else to send me. It was six months before they found a foster through the council. She was the one who registered me as mentally handicapped – just because she thought I was slow. I was – I'd missed school a lot. But I mean if she hadn't registered me, I would never have gone into institutions in the first place would I?

A pause. HARRY's not saying anything, listening, letting her talk.

Then from the foster I went to Kingsmead – part of the bin it is. I didn't know it was going to be. Make you into bin cases there they do. I was seventeen. I had a friend there I did who was sent to Severalls for ECT because she kept trying to jump out of the window. She had more than one course of ECT, but she ended up committing suicide while she was there anyway. See, they said they gave her ECT to stop her thinking about suicide – but the more ECT she had the more loss of memory she suffered and that gave her all the more reason for committing suicide. Bloody daft.

Still HARRY's listening, silently offers her a cigarette.

I gave it up. After Kingsmead I went to Lexden. A social worker took me there. I wouldn't have gone if I'd known that was going to be even more of a bin. Frightening it was there. I remember someone being sent to Rampton just because she was provoked. They made her eat one of her dinners that she didn't like – they were force feeding her and she hit one of the staff over the head with a plate, so then they sent her to Rampton. They said she was playing up and had to have a section of her brain removed. Only made her worse, poor cow. She kept having fits when she came back. They started giving me drugs when I was there too. They said I was depressed. I was. I hated the place. Only the drugs made me feel worse, so then I was sent to Essex Hall – a hospital for the subnormal. Give you treatment there if you play up – shock therapy – kills off the nerve cells so you'll forget. I know it does – there's chunks I still can't remember. Not that I want to anyway.

Pause as she makes tea, hands a cup to HARRY.

Take sugar?

HARRY: It's okay – there's some in it.

SHONA: There isn't.

HARRY: There is – it's sugared.

SHONA: There isn't any sugar in it.

HARRY: The tea's sugared.

SHONA: You can have some if you want.

HARRY: I promise you I've got sugar in this tea.

SHONA: I didn't sugar it.

HARRY: Well, someone did.

A pause.

You still on drugs?

SHONA: Course I'm not. I don't need them, do I? Don't worry. I won't freak out — chop you up.

HARRY: Lizzie Bowden.

SHONA: Oh yes.

HARRY: Lizzie Bowden took an axe, gave her mother thirty whacks; when she saw what she had done, she gave her father thirty-one.

SHONA: I remember that when I was a kid.

HARRY: And they never found out why she did it. Forty years of research and they put it down to it being ninety degrees in the shade and Lizzie's menstrual tensions.

SHONA: Oh really.

Quickly, compulsively she reaches forward, takes a fag, smokes like an old trooper. HARRY sees it, says nothing.

HARRY: Well, that's the caring profession of psychologists for you.

SHONA: Don't like 'em either do you?

HARRY: I don't like the morality — the philosophy they're hired to justify.

SHONA: Who hires them?

HARRY: Anyone with the readies. Church, politicians, philosophers, psychologists — they're all in it together.

SHONA: Wish I could have come out with that to shrinks I've seen. Might have let me go years ago.

HARRY: I doubt it. You could always have escaped though couldn't you?

SHONA: You think I didn't?

HARRY: But you went back.

SHONA: I had no where else to go did I? I was always running away. Where could I go? Everyone knew where you were from anyway, down in the village. You could see them looking at you and thinking. You don't believe me do you?

HARRY: You could have gone home or something.

SHONA: If I knew where home was. After I was twenty-one I didn't see my mother anymore. It wouldn't have made any difference anyway — she would have sent me back. She always did what the doctors told her. Who wouldn't, I suppose. They think you must be loony to think the medical profession could do anything wrong. They've had years of practice — who are we to question them? All that training they must be right.

HARRY: Bit angry underneath it all aren't you?

SHONA: Anger's not mad is it? Because I'm not on tranks that's why. That's what they do. Put you on tranks and take the fight out of you. Twelve years they took off me, what do you expect? Sometimes I wake up in the middle of the night no reason at all and I feel so angry I think my body will explode. Think I'm going to scream. Then I think well, maybe I am mad, because I haven't actually got anything to be angry about in the middle of the night have I? I just start feeling anxious and scared — about nothing — the fear of going insane and my mind racing and I start biting the blanket . . . hoping — hoping I live through it, morning will come, it'll be all right.

HARRY: It will be. In time. In the future.

SHONA: Yeah.

HARRY: Your choice now.

SHONA: Future that's penniless? No skills. I even got refused as a table clearer at the Odeon Leicester Square because they said I didn't have experience. That's not choice.

HARRY: Maybe you didn't want the job.

SHONA: Well, have you got a job?

HARRY: No.

SHONA: Well, there you are then.

HARRY: But it's choice. Rent free accommodation in the squat here.

SHONA: You need other money.

HARRY: I've got a few savings.

SHONA: You're lucky to have the choice then.

HARRY: You should be on top of the world.

SHONA: Too terrified for that. Can't believe I'm free. Think about all the others still there, crashing their brains against those iron bedsteads. Can't believe I'm twenty-eight. Feel almost like I'm suddenly going to be sixteen all over again.

HARRY: You don't have to worry. You'll learn to build. Confidence. It'll come.

SHONA: Hope so. Don't want to wait till I'm forty I don't.

Pause.

You're clever you are aren't you?

HARRY: Oh, that's me.

SHONA: I mean, you shouldn't be out of work, living here should you?

HARRY (*after a pause, in which he decides not to tell her anything about himself*): Well, like I said, it's what I choose.

SHONA: Don't still waters run deep then. You know, once there was an experiment at Lexden: it was mixed therapy, outpatients and inpatients, except some of the outpatients, most of them, were really just friends of the therapist. Like playing a game but it did them good I think. No one else knew what the fucking hell was going on.

HARRY (*smiles*): Said you were sub-normal did they?

SHONA: Oh, but I was highest. You were

graded, high, middle, low; then there was mongol and autistic. I was top of the bin I was.

HARRY: Yeah. I was senior sixer once.

SHONA: What?

HARRY: In the wolf cubs. Back in Attercliffe in Sheffield. Blue scarves and grand howls. I mean, we all move on — one thing to another.

Pause. A sudden spontaneous smile between them.

HARRY (*drinking tea*): Here's to the future then.

SHONA: Cheers.

Pause.

HARRY: How about dinner?

SHONA: Who?

HARRY: You. Saturday night . . .

SHONA: Where?

HARRY: What do you fancy? French? Italian?

SHONA: Is there a MacDonalds near here?

Scene Three

DR WALL *as before — flicks on his micro-recorder and working from the notes, dictates his lecture.*

DR WALL: Leeds University lecture — first section. Gentlemen — welcome. As most of you know, I am Dr Ian Wall, consultant psychiatrist, working with Dr Singer at the Brook General, and I have the job of delivering the first paper of our conference today. In giving the paper, I shall assume knowledge and background to our subject, and perhaps a certain common sentiment, free of the bias attached to more uninformed views. But let us be quite honest. Ours is not an easy task. The idea of irreversibly destroying living brain tissue as a last resort cure for psychiatric problems remains repellent even to many otherwise highly knowledgeable members of our profession Which is why I stress gentlemen, today we are no longer sticking a knife in the side of the brain and waggling it about – what used to be called the freehand pre-frontal. We do not deny it took place. In the dark old days I know it was performed as a cure for schizophrenia on a good ten thousand of our patients. If I may be allowed a reminiscence, I recall neurosurgeons doing at least ten pre-frontals in the morning and another ten in the afternoon. Just go down the line. £5 a time. Today we conceed this spate of leucotomies was a mistake – despite twenty per cent patients improving. Hundreds did get worse. Many died from haemorrhage. Yet the fact remains, even today, destruction of the nerve fibres linking the brain's active centres often can be the only way of curing those suffering desperate anxiety, depression, obsessional neurosis, and of making many altogether less aggressive. Those who every day see in their work, as I do in mine – who see every day in their work, as I do in mine – the very real misery of so many, will have little doubt as to the value of such operations. And fortunately today, I am able to say, only one third of psychosurgery still involves freehand knife sweeps. The greater number of our operations claim far more efficiency and, as many of you will know, are performed stereotactically; patient's head clamped in a calibrated vice or what not, enabling the surgeon to spear very specific spots in the brain with either electrodes or radio-active pellets. Possibly healthy brain tissue is still destroyed outside the specific area, but there is no doubt damage done is very much more controlled than it was. We are working today – gentlemen – on many fronts. In all, surgeons in forty-four different hospitals are making seventeen different types of lesion, in over fourteen parts of the brain – all

excellent work – which I shall detail – in the second part of my paper. (*He switches the micro-recorder off.*) And why not?

Scene Four

HARRY *and* SHONA *in the squat.*

HARRY: Not a bad launch into the future was it? Miss the main movie – get attacked on the way back by a madman.

SHONA: He wasn't mad was he.

HARRY: Till he saw us. He was screaming.

SHONA: He was scared. He just picked up on something.

HARRY: Not such a marvellous time though was it?

SHONA: We had the MacDonalds – I think they're a bloody luxury.

HARRY: Right. Land of milk, honey and MacDonalds – what more could you ask?

SHONA: What couldn't I?

HARRY: What?

SHONA: Everything I haven't got.

HARRY: House, garden, happy marriage?

SHONA: There's worse ways of living.

HARRY: There's got to be better too.

SHONA: Why?

HARRY: Marriage means exploitation doesn't it?

SHONA: How does it?

HARRY: When the old tribal chief started collecting the doweries, he then had to insure his line of inheritance. That meant insuring his women so he started this new thing called marriage. All bound up with property and profit you see. Wicked it is.

SHONA: It is if you haven't got it.

HARRY: I'm going to have to educate you.

SHONA: Oh, are you . . .

HARRY: One or two things . . .

SHONA: Like what?

HARRY: Ohh . . . the art of French cooking.

SHONA: Been around have you?

HARRY: Here and there. Who hasn't?

SHONA: Only place we ever went was sometimes to see a film. We'd all walk through the village, a long file of us walking in twos: first the girls, then the boys. Everybody would be looking at us and they'd know where we were from. It was horrible. And having to sit separately, boys from girls. They'd thought we'd want to kiss and cuddle only you weren't expected to have such feelings see.

Pause.

HARRY: But you did?

SHONA: What do you think?

Pause. Something between them.

SHONA: Not wrong is it?

HARRY: Wicked.

SHONA: Sound like them you do.

HARRY: Who?

SHONA: The whole lot. When I was out on the order, the care and protection order when I was fifteen, my mother was told she was incapable of looking after me — see, she'd let the lodger have sex with me.

HARRY: When you were fifteen?

SHONA: He'd raped me. And then me and my mum and him went to court and the magistrate asked if he'd done it against my will. I said yes — but my mother said she'd asked the lodger to have sex with me so that I wouldn't go out with other boys. She thought if I had sex with him, I wouldn't want to go with anyone else.

HARRY: Unbelievable. What happened to the lodger?

SHONA: He went home with my mum — then when the case came up he went to court. I wasn't there mind — and they said he had to go to prison, but my mum said it wasn't his fault, and he was allowed to go home with her again.

HARRY: And you were away in the remand home?

SHONA: I felt really bad. I did.

HARRY: Jesus.

SHONA (*after a pause, and anxious to move on*): Tell me how old you are?

HARRY: Guess.

SHONA: Older than me.

HARRY: Right.

SHONA: Thirty.

HARRY: No.

SHONA: You look it.

HARRY: You don't look 28.

SHONA: Thirty-three.

HARRY: Thirty-two.

SHONA: Thirty-two?

HARRY: Old enough.

SHONA: Can't imagine you being young. A kid I mean.

HARRY: Sometimes go back to Attercliffe — where I grew up. Feel like someone's going to tap me on the shoulder and say 'That's it mate — your time's up. You're back here now — you stay here.'

SHONA: Didn't you like it?

HARRY: Something I didn't like about it. Wasn't just the endless roofs, the backyard, the old man, the way they started dropping the terraced houses overnight. Wasn't much hope. Wanted something different.

SHONA: Still do then?

HARRY: You bet.

SHONA: But what happened in-between?

HARRY: Things that didn't work.

SHONA: That you don't want to remember tonight.

HARRY: Yeah.

SHONA: I can't remember much of my childhood at all. Not the early part. It goes, you just forget after the shock treatment. Great blanks in the end.

HARRY: Why d'you say they give it to you?

SHONA: Sometimes they say you're playing up; sometimes they say you're depressed. The drugs they give you, you don't know what's going on anyway.

HARRY: But you don't have to be raving.

SHONA: You're worried aren't you – I'll start screaming.

HARRY: Well, it's my fear. I mean I'm not really – I don't see enough good ad's for sanity the way we are.

SHONA: What d'you think you'd do if you were mad then?

HARRY: I am.

SHONA: Seriously.

HARRY: Rape women.

SHONA: Don't have to be mad.

HARRY: Freak out – bash my head against the wall – kill – murder. If I was mad – let go – fall in love – feel.

SHONA: Fall in love.

HARRY: What?

Pause.

You all right?

SHONA: Yes.

Pause.

HARRY: It doesn't have to be a big heavy thing between us. I can go to my own room.

SHONA: What's wrong. I want to.

HARRY: Oh. Well, that's all right then.

SHONA: It is all right, isn't it?

HARRY: What?

SHONA: Well, I don't know you.

HARRY: You know me.

A pause.

SHONA: Is it all right?

HARRY: It's all right.

SHONA: Honestly?

HARRY: Stop it, Shona.

SHONA: I'd hate it, if it wasn't all right.

Scene Five

HARRY *and* SHONA *lying somewhere together in the almost darkened squat.*

HARRY: You okay?

SHONA: Like America it is here . . . It's what I used to think – about going to America – being in a car and driving across the open spaces. Texas. I used to imagine I was arriving in Carolina at midnight, in the hospital . . . when I wished I wasn't alive, didn't know my body because it had changed so – I used to think one day I'll do that; get there; like a church I'd go in . . . it was always there.

HARRY: Never stopping – that's the real trick; stop and it's so difficult to go on. Feel rooted. Think you can shake them off you know, but I don't know it's even in the nature of the beast.

SHONA: What you talking about Harry?

HARRY: I don't know. Making something new; getting there; getting away. Being there. Alive.

Long pause.

SHONA: Why you with me Harry?

HARRY: Because you're mad.

Pause.

SHONA: But I'm not – am I?

HARRY: You know what I mean. I mean, you're not chained in sanity, wanting it like everyone else.

SHONA: Thought I did.

HARRY: Yes, but thinking it and having it, they're different. You're exciting – anything could happen – I feel alive, not dead.

SHONA: Sounds freaky.

Pause.

HARRY: What are you doing?

SHONA: Worrying if I'll get to sleep.

HARRY: Why?

SHONA: I just do. Start thinking. Everything around seems strange. Being here with you. Like I don't know where I am – no reason. It's all a big film set. Something behind the walls. A director watching us all.

HARRY: Well, maybe.

SHONA: Scary to think about.

Pause.

I don't want to go back again, one thing I know. I heard of a woman who went into a bin when she was eighteen and she didn't get out till she went to an old people's home when she was sixty-eight. Fifty years. She just got lost. Like a life isn't it? All those years I was inside and I still don't know who I am. Lying here. Did you ever think – what's a body – that it was nothing to do with you?

HARRY: Go to sleep.

SHONA: I know. But I can't. Mind just races, I've so much energy. Suppose it's all that time I didn't do anything, all those drugs. Feel I could run a marathon. You don't fancy coming for a run in the park?

HARRY: At three o'clock in the morning?

SHONA: Why not?

HARRY: Shona.

SHONA: What's that!?

HARRY: What?

SHONA: Sticking out of the wall?

HARRY: What?

SHONA: There.

HARRY: It's the old wiring.

SHONA: Looks horrible.

HARRY: Close your eyes. Come on . . .

Pause.

SHONA: Can't lie here. I don't even know you. Just a man.

HARRY: Come on.

SHONA: Sing me to sleep.

HARRY: I don't know any songs.

Pause.

SHONA: 'Once upon a time . . . that little girl . . .'

Pause.

Glad my name's not Lizzie I am . . .

Pause.

Lizzie Bowden took an axe – gave her mother thirty whacks. When she saw what she had done – she gave her father . . . thirty one . . .

Scene Six

Tape: violent, primal scream from SHONA, *with the voice of two men and one woman cutting in.*

1ST MAN: Shona, stop it!

WOMAN: Grab her arm.

2ND MAN: Hold her down!

SHONA *continues screaming, shouting abuse.*

Scene Seven

HARRY *and* SHONA *in the bin.*
SHONA'*s hair is in a bit of a mess where
she's had a go at cutting it. They are
seated across a table, staring silently at
each other.*

SHONA (*at length*): Fuck off!

HARRY: Shona, it's me.

SHONA: Fuck off!

HARRY: You don't mean that Shona –
I came here to help you.

SHONA: How are you then? Looking
a bit white, Harry.

HARRY: That's being here, isn't it.

SHONA: Nervous?

HARRY: Sure I'm nervous. Put you to
the test, these places. So what
happened, Shona?

SHONA: Keep your voice down.

HARRY: What happened? I came back –
the others said you'd freaked out –

SHONA: They fucking well attacked me
and they know they did.

HARRY: I honestly thought everything
was fine – out for a meal the night
before.

SHONA: Oh yes.

HARRY: So I went out for a walk in
the morning. I needed to spend time
alone. You're not the only one with
a past you know. You were asleep.
I needed to think.

SHONA: Took your fucking time.

HARRY: But what were you doing in
my room Shona?

SHONA: Cutting my hair.

HARRY: I know –

SHONA: I'm sure you like short haired
women don't you, Harry?

HARRY: They said if they hadn't
stopped you, you would have cut it
all off.

SHONA: What's it got to do with
them? Course I wouldn't cut it all off.
Just an experiment.

HARRY: They said you were manic.
That's why they tried to stop you.

SHONA: They attacked me. Why?

HARRY: They tried to find out what
was wrong; you threatened them with
the scissors and attacked them. They
were scared. They thought you'd
flipped. Why Shona – they said here
you even threw an armchair through
the television screen last night – why?

SHONA: Why did they inject me? And
why refuse to give me my clothes?
Where are my clothes now? Why
haven't I got my clothes? Can I have
my clothes back please!

HARRY: Shona.

SHONA: Ignore me deliberately. They're
watching me though. I know.

HARRY: Who is?

SHONA: These blacks in here.

HARRY: They're staff.

SHONA: They don't trust me.

HARRY: Well, you did throw a fucking
armchair through the television screen.
Look at it from their point.

SHONA: Tell me I'm supposed to rest.
How am I supposed to rest in this
bin if they're watching me all the
time.

HARRY: They're not.

SHONA: They follow me around as if I
was one of these loony patients here.

HARRY: You're imagining it. It's part
of being here, Shona.

SHONA: Then why is she over there
behind me now?

HARRY: But she's not watching you.

SHONA: You must be mad. That
woman is watching me.

HARRY: She's just doing her job. Why

should she be watching you? If you watch her — yes, she'll watch you.

SHONA: Am I watching her now? She is watching me.

HARRY: Why should she?

SHONA: She wants control.

HARRY: Jesus, you think she hasn't got enough to worry about in her own life?

SHONA: She's evil. That's why.

HARRY: What does that mean?

SHONA: God's punishment.

HARRY: Shona, that's madness. Don't you recognise it?

SHONA: How is it?

HARRY: God isn't a force that punishes.

SHONA: Not so loudly. I'm warning you. If you say anything they don't want —

HARRY: All right.

SHONA: God controls everything.

HARRY: Yes?

SHONA: There you are then.

HARRY: What?

SHONA: If he wants to punish me, he'll use the blacks. Everything that happens has a reason — I didn't meet you by chance.

HARRY: Of course it was chance.

SHONA: Everything that happens is part of God's pattern. The woman in Camden Town. With her bags. She's not forgotten.

HARRY: I'm not with you.

SHONA: You don't see it do you Harry? I see it. It's happening all over. People are blind.

HARRY: What's happening?

SHONA: The evil. Punishment. Meted out.

HARRY: Shona, why should you be punished?

SHONA: For being born.

HARRY: You're not making sense.

SHONA: If we didn't have sin we wouldn't be born. God would save us.

HARRY: What do you think God is?

SHONA: You tell me.

HARRY: Well, he isn't a big man with a stick or a whip is he? I mean, he doesn't exist outside there somewhere — he's the sum of us all — he's there — in the flowers — in the trees.

SHONA: God in the trees! Ha, ha ha!

HARRY: Shona.

SHONA: Were they listening? Do you think they heard?

HARRY: No one is listening. We're not that important.

SHONA: Not even to God?

HARRY: All right — to God.

SHONA: There you are then.

HARRY: What?

SHONA: He's chosen to punish me.

HARRY: Look you freaked out back at the house.

SHONA: Last night it felt as if flames were licking over my flesh.

HARRY: After the injection?

SHONA: Did I ask for it? Did I ask to be brought here?

Pause.

There's some fucking mad people here, Harry.

HARRY: You're telling me — I'm mad — I think we're all fucking mad.

SHONA: You're not mad.

HARRY: God isn't punishing you for being mad — you're no madder than the rest of us.

SHONA: How are you mad?

HARRY: What isn't mad? I don't believe you're insane okay? Mixed up.

Who wouldn't be in a bin. It's
infectious.

SHONA: But you don't believe I'm mad?

HARRY: You're not a raving loony,
no. Being in these places how do you
know you're sane anyway? I mean,
what's sane? Being here, see people
freaking out, there aren't any limits.
What are my limits? How do I know
I won't go over the top? So if you
do go over the top — what's the
difference here? Outside there are a
thousand little guidelines — points of
security. You believe in them. It's
a way of interpreting the world and
getting along. But in here don't even
I look mad? Look at my hand —
shaking like the clappers, like the
controls are all off — you don't know
what's going to happen.

SHONA: The doctors aren't mad.

HARRY: Well, they can't afford to
admit the possibility of an alternative,
can they? They'd really go fucking
crazy.

SHONA: Don't use that language in front
of me, if you don't mind.

HARRY: Oh, Shona, look —

SHONA: And you realise they heard
every word you said.

HARRY: Look, I'm going to have to go
in a moment. I mean, what do you
want to do?

SHONA: No choice is there? I'm a
prisoner here if that's what you mean.

HARRY: They can't keep you here
against your will.

SHONA: If I'm not a prisoner why am I
locked up here?

HARRY: You're not locked up.

SHONA: Then why are the doors locked?

HARRY: Are the doors locked? I don't
know why the doors are locked.

SHONA: They lock them as soon as the
visitors go.

HARRY: Well, perhaps there are some
people safer here than outside. Shona,
you want to come back with me,
okay. I'll look after you. Look, it
didn't mean nothing you know,
Saturday night. What do you want
to do?

SHONA: I'm supposed to be ill.

HARRY: You're not ill, Maybe they
say you're ill — you were perfectly
all right.

A pause.

SHONA: All right. I'll get my clothes.

*She walks off, a bit zombie like.
In a moment HARRY goes after her.*

(Off:) These are my clothes —
give me my clothes, I want my
clothes you fucking cow — give me
my fucking clothes — I want to go
home!

*A simultaneous slap, scream, and
black out.*

Scene Eight

HARRY *with* DR WALL.

DR WALL (*with a file*): How long had
you been in contact with her?

HARRY: How long had I known her?

DR WALL: Yes.

HARRY: A few days — since she came
to the house.

DR WALL: Yes. And that's where she
started behaving violently?

HARRY: Apparently.

DR WALL: Didn't she?

HARRY: Maybe she felt provoked. She
says she was.

DR WALL: Her attack on the nurse
wasn't provoked.

HARRY: She wouldn't give her her
clothes.

DR WALL: She wasn't entitled to them.

HARRY: You're entitled to yours –

DR WALL: Look –

HARRY: Why don't you just let her go home?

DR WALL: She's seriously ill.

HARRY: She's uptight about being in here.

DR WALL: I've seen many patients such as her. Without the attention of trained personnel we should witness further rapid deterioration of her condition.

HARRY: Until she got here she didn't have a condition.

DR WALL: You must be aware she has a case history as long as your arm. She'll probably live with her illness the rest of her life short of some drastic development.

HARRY: Because you have a file on her doesn't make her a nutcase. I'm not accepting that. That's your file – that's all.

DR WALL: Look, I do understand: an initial contact with mental illness can be a very frightening experience.

HARRY: If she's mentally ill.

DR WALL: She's been in centres and subnormal institutes practically all her life.

HARRY: She told me. Since she was raped.

DR WALL: That's not in the file.

HARRY: That's what she told me.

DR WALL (*from file*): Age sixteen, placed under care and protection after exhibiting signs of promiscuity. Fostered at seventeen – outbreaks of violence. Registered mentally handicapped and placed in care. Condition deteriorates – further violent outbursts – removal to Essex Hall – diagnosis follows as a paranoid schizophrenic. Various treatments – prolonged course of ECT –

HARRY: Look, whatever your file says – whatever happened back at the house – she's still a human being. Confused – unsophisticated – okay –

DR WALL: She can also be quite dangerous. Set fire to a wing of Essex Hall. She's made numerous attacks on staff.

HARRY: I can't say I blame her for that.

DR WALL: You know you're not helping her. She's sick, man. There are doctors, nurses here, in hospitals all over the country, giving their lives to helping people like her. Now we can't really do anything for her until we know what the precipitating factors were – and that's where you could help. We can't talk to her until she comes down. That's why we gave her medication when she came in. All right it hasn't worked – we'll increase the dosage.

HARRY: Without her consent.

DR WALL: We're not treating her against her will – this is not a prison.

HARRY: Look, I know she's been disturbed – she needs care – looking after.

DR WALL: Isn't that what she's here for? You want to help her, help us. Before her disturbance, tell me how she was behaving?

HARRY: She was normal, bit scatty maybe.

DR WALL: Was she?

HARRY: I wasn't there when she's supposed to have freaked out. I don't know what happened.

DR WALL: No strangeness, withdrawal – even hysteria – the night before.

HARRY: No.

DR WALL: Was she having sex?

HARRY: What's that got to do with it?

DR WALL: Was she on medication?

HARRY: You make it sound like hot chocolate. No she wasn't. She didn't need it.

DR WALL: Obviously she did. According to her records she should have been on medication.

HARRY: She said she didn't need it.

DR WALL: Did she sleep with you before her outbreak?

HARRY: I don't see what that's got to do with it.

DR WALL: Sleeping with anyone would place her under enormous stress — a highly charged, complex act for her to undertake.

HARRY: Well, I thought it was natural. So did she.

DR WALL: And the disturbance took place the next day?

HARRY: So it's all my fault is it?

DR WALL: I realise it must be difficult for you to accept a healthy act between two normal people can bring about such disastrously unhealthy results in this young lady's case.

HARRY: That still assumes she's sick. Your assumption.

DR WALL: Very well. I don't think we're going to make any progress until we've brought her down and can talk to her. I'm sorry. Three days and we'll see. Let her get some rest. Safe place for her here.

HARRY: But she doesn't want to stay does she?

DR WALL: On the safe side. Three days. Just observation.

HARRY: You've already pumped her full of drugs.

DR WALL: It's in her best interests. She's in no condition to leave.

HARRY: She's had twelve years of bins and she hates them. Give her her clothes and let her go.

DR WALL: Mr Phillips, under Section 30 of the Mental Health Act patients entering asylum of their own free will, then changing their minds, can be held for three days, with or without medical examination. That's the law. She was admitted voluntarily and I think it's in her best interests that she stays.

HARRY: That's it then.

DR WALL: I'm sorry, Mr Phillips.

HARRY: Thank you.

Scene Nine

SHONA *in the bin after increased dosage. Looks as if she isn't seeing properly, and she's a bit stiff, except for the hands which shake.*

SHONA: They're poisoning me. These people here. They are. They've been poisoning me since I came here. And not just me — I phoned the health authorities. I told them. Someone has to protect them here. And if it's not true why did they put me in solitary confinement? As a punishment when they found out. You don't believe me. You think it's part of my illness. They put me in solitary confinement last night. It's a room down the corridor. Oh you think it's my paranoia. They locked the door. Why? Nothing but a bed. Piss yourself. Say it's another sign you're ill. Who said I was ill? Did I say I was ill? Do you think I'm ill? How do you know you're not ill? You might be ill? You don't know you're ill. Am I ill or are you ill? You're ill. You're not normal. You're in league with the devil. They're in league with the devil. You think I'm in league with the devil — you're ill. They are — trying to see I burn in hell. Look (*She shows a rash on a large part of her torso.*) They did that. Injected it into my blood. Trying to get rid of me. You don't believe me? You're ill. (*Pause. Then quiet:*) Smothering me. Tying me in knots . . . they are. (*She freezes as* DR WALL *enters.*)

DR WALL: Hello Shona. How are you liking it here?

SHONA: I'm not ill. I'm being poisoned, sir.

DR WALL: Is that why you phoned the health authorities?

SHONA: I am, sir.

DR WALL: Why do you say that, Shona?

SHONA: I get dizzy. I can't always see properly and my muscles feel all stiff. And I've come out in a rash.

DR WALL: We're sorry about the rash — but it's just a side effect in a course of treatment which we hope will make you better.

SHONA: It's the injections, sir.

DR WALL: They're to stop you feeling ill.

SHONA: I felt all right before I had them, sir.

DR WALL: Doesn't mean you weren't already ill, Shona, does it? You probably don't realise you're ill — part of the problem,

SHONA: Is it, sir?

DR WALL: You have to trust us. Remember, mistrust is just another symptom of the illness.

SHONA: But the drugs do make me feel ill. Like poison.

DR WALL: You mustn't think like that if you want to get better. You must trust.

SHONA: I was better before I was given the drugs.

DR WALL: Shona, haven't you seen people here who are too ill to know they're ill? Now before the drugs, you may have *said* you felt fine — but that may simply be because you weren't motivated to regain your health. I'm

sure other doctors have tried to explain schizophrenia to you haven't they? Remember, the patients who get better quickest are those who accept they are ill. Those who accept their treatment. There are people like you — outside now — living normal lives — still on treatment — but that's because they accept it is the only way they can lead normal, decent lives.

Pause.

I don't frighten you, do I?

SHONA: I mustn't offend you, sir.

DR WALL: Why not?

SHONA: You have the power to decide my fate, sir.

DR WALL: Is that what you really think?

SHONA: Otherwise I would go home, sir.

DR WALL: Shona, why do you always call me sir?

SHONA: Perhaps — because you're a messenger, sir — from God, sir. Come to tell me if I'm going to go to heaven or hell. Will it help my chances if I tell you the truth? If I confess how many times I've sinned, will it? Or will it make it worse?

DR WALL: It'll be all right, Shona. These things take time remember. But it'll be all right in the end. I'll have a look at your treatment — see what else we can do. See you again.

He leaves.

SHONA: Thinks he's God, he does. Stupid bastard.

Scene Ten

The DOCTOR *settles himself in his winged chair. Pours himself a glass of wine. Drinks. Rolls it around his mouth. Puts down the glass and, looking at his notes on the wine table, picks up his micro-recorder and switches it on.*

DR WALL: Section two — anxiety, repeated violence, obsessional neurosis, schizophrenia, self-destructive behaviour, anorexia nervosa — many other complaints — all of them symptoms which may be relieved by psychosurgery today. Today at the Brook for example, we are treating the chronically depressed — all of whom have already undergone prolonged courses of drugs and ECT — with what is called a subcaudate tractotomy, where brain tissue in the subcaudate region, between the frontal lobe and the hypothalamus — roughly just behind the eyes — is destroyed by placing 7mm long radioactive yttrium rods through a narrow incision in the forehead. The activated yttrium rods destroy an area of brain about — oh, 22mm by 6mm, size of a square of chocolate perhaps. Destruction of tissue separates the caring and judgement centres of the frontal lobe from the more instinctual, deeply rooted hypothalamus, thereby breaking the viscious circuit of tension that patients develop. Work of a slightly different nature is carried out at the Atkinson Morley by our colleagues Drs Kray and Kelly. They are engaged with suicide patients and introduce some seven electrodes into two parts of the brain — the lower medial quadrant and the cingulate — destroying tissue by heat coagulation.

Pause.

Most controversial of all work is the amygdalotomie, carried out by Dr West at Edinburgh. This as its name implies involves destroying the amygdala, part of the brain's older, instinctive rhombic system —

performed exclusively on aggressive patients and epileptics to permanently passify them. Surgery involves drilling a hole in the side of the skull just in front of the ear, and then inserting electrodes to coagulate and destroy the tissue. Not as simple as it sounds since the brain has first to be stimulated with an electric current in order that the amygdala or seat of aggression as it is sometimes called, can be correctly located. This means of course patients must remain conscious and during this part of the operation many become very disturbed. Three angry patients . . .

Pause.

Three patients are reported to have escaped altogether and the whole thing has had to be called off. The aim of the operation of course is to reduce such violent behaviour. Accepting aggression depends on specific social situations, where it is not possible to remove these, the symptom itself is removed. And Dr West reports that after operations, patients have returned to the same situation with few of the same responses. Indication I think of total success, gentlemen. I know overall in our work, there are those who object, who say we are knocking them off — I know the arguments. I have spent many, many hours in my consulting room with distressed relatives of patients, convincing them of the value of our work — a value I hope will in future be better appreciated — and is not least the purpose of our conference today.

He pauses, thinks.

Scene Eleven

HARRY *waiting in the bin.* SHONA *enters. She's drugged up to the eyeballs. Moves slowly. Shakes. Sits. Crosses her leg as if it's a delicate operation. But then barely for a second, throughout the scene, can she stop the foot twitching. She doesn't say anything.* HARRY *is shocked: here she is: a real live mad mental patient.*

HARRY: How are you Shona?

She nods her head a little.

HARRY: You look awful.

Pause. As throughout the scene, there are long moments when HARRY *can't find a handle to get in; but in the silence he has a sense he's still giving to her; maybe now it's the most he can give her.*

SHONA (*at length*): Come to take me home have you?

HARRY: Have you seen the doctor?

SHONA: No. Oh yes. I did.

HARRY: What did he say?

SHONA: Nothing.

Pause. Then she looks off. Her eyes narrow.

Fuck off!

HARRY: So who was that?

SHONA: Fucking maniac. Creeping around for days.

Long pause.

HARRY: Has it been really bad in here?

SHONA: Drive you round the bend.

HARRY: Do you know when you're seeing the doctor again or what's happening?

SHONA: Nothing happens. Stay here.

HARRY: Are you seeing me, Shona?

SHONA (*sudden smile*): Course I can see you. Why do you ask?

HARRY: You don't look well. You look worse than when I saw you before.

SHONA: What d'you expect. Why I've got to get out of here.

HARRY: Do you really — would you be all right outside?

SHONA: This is the drugs — not a sign I'm ill. Wasn't like this before was I? Well, do you think I'm ill, honestly, do you?

HARRY: You're not in the best of health, Shona, that's for sure.

SHONA: Read you the records did they?

HARRY: What?

SHONA: Don't want a paranoid schizophrenic living with you I suppose.

HARRY: Shona, we all already knew about you.

SHONA: But not a real living mad one.

HARRY: What happened Shona?

SHONA: What? The fire?

HARRY: Back at the house, the fire, what happens?

SHONA: An accident. Wasn't my fault there were no unlocked fire exits.

Long pause.

(*Quieter:*) Trying. Trying to think I'm in America. Know I'm not really.

Pause.

Did they say why I couldn't have my clothes.

HARRY: They think you'll run away.

SHONA: Longer you stay here everything gets further away. Put in here, try to pretend you don't exist.

HARRY: I've asked to see the doctor again. I'll speak to him, find out what's going on. Someone around here must be concerned.

SHONA: Rather be in a prison. Least you know when you're getting out.

Pause.

Do you believe there's anything wrong with me Harry? I mean do you believe I'm mad?

HARRY: What's madness, Shona? Something's disturbed you – we know that. I'll see the doctor. Wait till then, Shona.

SHONA: Get out of here. Go to New York or somewhere.

They sit there awhile in silence. HARRY disblieving the whole situation a little.

Scene Twelve

HARRY *and* the DOCTOR.

DR WALL: Let me explain – paranoid schizophrenia is a disease due mainly to an inherent biochemical defect. Despite all the other well-intentioned theories put forward that's what it remains. Your new theories are all well and good but it doesn't stop 'em piling up in the wards does it? Doesn't actually help them.

HARRY: But I don't see that you're helping her either. No one attempts to understand her.

DR WALL: But what the inherent defect does is to scatter the logic – separates the body, feelings, the head – making sense, understanding the madness wouldn't solve anything. The important understanding is to discover why the illness has appeared now. I suspect it's because the sexual excitement of her relationship with you has stressed her delicate state. Why, a stay in hospital's a good place for her. Rules forbid sexual contact – she knows that – gives her security – a chance to rest. At the moment we don't know why she's behaving as she is. There are no simple explanations.

HARRY: But her behaviour is in line with your treatment – I mean the treatment makes her exhibit all the signs you diagnose as schizophrenia.

DR WALL: You cannot accept she is ill can you? That she'll carry her illness with her all her life.

HARRY: No, I can't.

DR WALL: Well, I'm afraid it's true.

HARRY: I don't accept madness is some strange force we can't understand. They're helpless people – to say she's mad – doesn't mean you can wash your hands – oh, it's easier – helping, bothering, might mean you really had to give something of yourself.

DR WALL: And suppose she remained mad. Suppose your efforts had little or no effect? It happens. Madness is a fact – or the phenomena is a fact. Has been throughout history. It's not just a symptom of our illness which a few kind words will put right.

HARRY: It would take more than that.

DR WALL: Which is exactly what we're trying to do here.

HARRY: But as you progressively increase your treatment she gets steadily worse.

DR WALL: We had to add a second tranquilliser.

HARRY: And now I suppose you'll try another.

DR WALL: Possibly. Possibly we might try something else altogether.

HARRY: Try letting her go.

DR WALL: You don't really believe that would work. You think if we opened the hospitals and turned out all the patients we should see a thousand miraculous cures?

HARRY: I'm talking about her.

DR WALL: I understand how you feel. You saw her – someone who appeared perfectly normal – suddenly out of her mind. Of course you want to do the one thing that would set her on the right tracks again.

HARRY: Right.

DR WALL: And in panic situations one grabs the first solution to offer itself. She scares the shit out of you because she puts you in touch with your chaos, then she says, get me out of here, and effectively promises peace will reign again. But do you really think it would? Do you know what it's like living with a mental patient? Have you any idea how the necessary order of your life would be engulfed by the chaos of hers? You may get something out of it for a day — may help your liberal conscience — keep your adrenalin running. Longer, and she'll take you with her into insanity. Oh, it happens. Your fight's not with me or with the hospital. Your anger stems from your understandable fear. Be angry, be angry with her.

HARRY: How can you be angry with her. She's helpless.

DR WALL: Exactly. Which is why we must work together. If we can help her, you will no longer feel threatened, and no longer angry. Follow?

HARRY: So what's the answer?

DR WALL: We have all sorts of contingency treatments. We'll try them. We're really *not* villains. We like to see the world a better place. You see them in there, morbid, clap of the devil on them, some of them. We work to get them back in the mainstream. Sometimes it doesn't work. Very often it does. A lot of people walking the streets today on maintenance ECT — pop in for a dose once a week — lead perfectly normal lives. And couldn't otherwise. We try our best. But we can't solve all the world's problems. Worry yourself like you have been and you'll upset your own equilibrium. Find yourself in a bin. The hospitals are here for your protection as well. If there is a way of helping Shona we'll find it. It's no pleasure for me — pump someone full of drugs, refer them for ECT or surgery. Sometimes it has to be done.

It honestly wouldn't work to discharge her.

HARRY: Even I can see it's gone too far for that.

DR WALL: So if you want to help her and yourself, the most you can do is to encourage her to give up her rebelliousness — to trust us — to trust whatever recommendations we might make for treatment.

HARRY: Sounds like you've made some.

DR WALL: Not yet.

HARRY: But you will.

DR WALL: We have to. Accept she's ill. She can't. But that's the biggest obstacle to treatment.

HARRY: And if she just left of her own accord?

DR WALL: Do you believe that would help her?

HARRY: No.

DR WALL: And it's not possible anyway. After a second opinion, I'm afraid she's been placed under Section 25 — an order made in the interests of her own health and safety and the protection of others.

HARRY: What do you mean?

DR WALL: Myself and a colleague have signed the recommendation to the effect she's suffering from mental disorder and will be held for twenty-eight days.

HARRY: That's the law?

DR WALL: Absolutely.

Scene Thirteen

SHONA *in the bin.* SHONA *waits.* HARRY *enters with grapes. She raises a hand, waves as if from a long distance away.*

HARRY: Hi. How are you.

She nods, smiles. A pause.

SHONA: The same.

HARRY: Did the doctor see you? He said he would.

SHONA: Nice man.

HARRY: What did he say?

SHONA (*shakes her head. Pause. Then shrugs*): Said I was on the road to recovery I think. Said he'd look at my treatment.

Looks off. Rises. Moves to sit closer to HARRY. *Speaks very confidentially.*

Er, Harry — ssch — something I want to ask you. The room. Is the room all right? I'm worried about the room.

HARRY: This room —

SHONA: Ssch. At the house.

HARRY: It's yours.

She nods. Takes it in. Moves her chair back. Sits 'normally' again.

The room is yours. Everyone feels bad about what's happened. They do. They're concerned — they want to support you. We discussed it over supper. We're going to help look after you. We'll give you all the support you need, Shona. That's honestly what we want to do.

She looks at him, nodding. Then she's almost crying.

SHONA: Can't go on here, Harry. Fighting. The more I struggle, the tighter the knots get.

HARRY: Then don't struggle, Shona. I mean, why resist, if they're holding you? If you've got to stay a month — treat it like a hotel — have a good rest. So it's not five star — give the space to yourself to rest — you need it. And you deserve it, Shona.

A pause. She looks at the grapes. Flicks them with sudden disdain.

SHONA: Don't mind the rest. Don't want the treatment tomorrow.

HARRY: What treatment?

SHONA: Therapy. Charge nurse said this morning I was on the list.

HARRY: For ECT? What did he say?

SHONA: Treating me like some patient. 'You'll come and hear the music tomorrow — a special pair of phones for you.' Think they're gods with those machines. Just a punishment for playing up.

HARRY: They wouldn't do that, Shona — not unless it was recommended by the doctor.

SHONA: Because I saw them undressing someone and tying them down to the bed, and told them I'd write to my MP and untied her.

HARRY: What happened?

SHONA: They dragged her by the hair to the sick ward — injected her to keep her quiet. Told me it was my turn for the music tomorrow — I was on the list.

HARRY: But they meant the doctor's list surely.

SHONA: Why? Doctors don't do it. They do it all. 'Give 'em a good dose and get it over with!'

HARRY: Yes, but the doctor must have recommended it.

SHONA: I didn't ask for it. Done no good before. Kill a few more brain cells.

HARRY: Maybe it will work this time?

SHONA: You think I need it.

HARRY: I don't know, Shona. I don't know. And you don't know what the answer is do you?

SHONA: Answer to what?

HARRY: Shona, I can't stand seeing you like this. Anything's worth a try isn't it?

Pause.

I don't know . . . They're not ogres here. They've no vested interest in locking people up for long periods have they? Why not have the treatment. Who knows. Maybe you'll be back at the house by the weekend. They're doing what they can, aren't they? You have to help things work.

Long pause.

Look, maybe you have to accept you are ill, Shona.

SHONA: I'm not.

HARRY: But you don't feel – right – do you?

SHONA (*closing her eyes, head*): You think I haven't been through all this before. Talk of living on tablets the rest of my life. Sometimes I get bad-tempered, I will admit that. That's the only thing that's wrong with me. I don't know why. Shouldn't have thought I just woke up one day feeling angry, I mean, something else must have happened before that to make me angry.

HARRY: We're talking about now – living now.

SHONA: I wish I was dead.

Pause.

HARRY: Made any friends here?

SHONA: One woman you can talk to. You?

HARRY: What?

SHONA: What you been doing?

HARRY: Oh, cleaning up.

SHONA: Visiting friends?

HARRY: No.

Pause.

Have the treatment. Try it. See.

Pause.

SHONA: Suppose I must be ill.

Scene Fourteen

DR WALL *seated in his winged chair, notes laid aside as he puts back his head, closes his eyes, and with exquisite concentration, listens to some highly refined piece of music. Music mixes (as lights fade) with interference – mixes with increasing interference – until the static alone sounds and becomes an electronic effect depicting the popular nightmare of ECT: a short, screaming burst of current as it jolts through the brain.*

Scene Fifteen

SHONA *in the bin.*

SHONA: I think I was feeling oppressed. I was. It's all right now though. I mean, I'm all right, I am. I get these headaches – but it's all right: doesn't mean you're mad because you have ECT. Just go in and come out really. Strap your chest and ankles down and put these headphones on you. Then they give you an injection – next you're waking up and they're giving you oxygen. Then you get sent off to have a cup of tea. And you're feeling all right. More or less. You tend to forget a bit. I remember being at Harry's. I can't remember after that. I mean, there's a chunk of last week I can't remember – if it was last week. The headaches started this week. After the treatment – but it's just a side effect. I can't really remember what happened at the squat. Suppose it doesn't matter – whatever it was – someone who doesn't mind me being in the bin and that, I'm lucky I am. And the headaches have got to be a sign the treatment's working, haven't they? Even if you do lose your memory. They told me I'd smashed the television. You can't go around smashing televisions I suppose, can you? Televisions cost a lot of money. I've got to be on good behaviour anyway, I have, for when I see the doctor. Don't know about going home if you're not. Might even send me off to Severalls. That's the next step all right. And we all know what happens there.

DR WALL enters. She begins to behave immediately as if she's guilty, and wants to conceal this.

DR WALL: Ah. How are we feeling then? Better?

SHONA: Still got a headache, sir.

DR WALL: We'll give you something for that. Won't last anyway.

SHONA: Then can I go home, sir?

DR WALL: Tell me how you're feeling — apart from the headaches.

SHONA: All right.

DR WALL: Know what brought it all on?

SHONA: What?

DR WALL: No, you have to tell me. What was going on — before your friends brought you in here.

SHONA (*after pause*): I was sitting on the floor that's all. I was cutting my hair.

DR WALL: You were cutting it all off. Why?

SHONA: I was waiting for Harry.

DR WALL: It was his room.

SHONA: With his pictures in it.

DR WALL: Humm?

SHONA: An album, I was looking at it.

DR WALL: Yes?

SHONA: Looked through it, then I was sitting thinking about it. Then I started cutting my hair. That's all.

DR WALL: What aren't you telling me, Shona?

SHONA: I don't remember.

DR WALL: Shona, if you want to go home . . .

SHONA: Photographs of his wife, children.

DR WALL (*after pause*): How did you feel?

SHONA: Nothing.

DR WALL: Nothing?

SHONA: No.

DR WALL: And now?

SHONA: I've got this headache.

DR WALL: I told you we'll give you something for that.

SHONA: And then can I go home, sir?

DR WALL: Where is home, Shona?

SHONA: Well, I mean — I don't know. It's a home.

DR WALL: Squat isn't it? Not much of a home — threat of eviction hanging over you.

SHONA: It is home, sir.

DR WALL: Wouldn't find the support of a proper family would you? Damp. Old mattress on the floor. That's not looking after yourself, is it?

SHONA: When can I go home, sir?

DR WALL (*rising*): We'll see. I'll get you something for that headache first. Don't worry — these things take their time, Shona. You should know that by now. I'll see you again.

He leaves. She sits in silence a long time.

SHONA: Said he'd let me go home, he did. Before I had the treatment. I remember that. Just before. Called me in.

She sits, spirit broken.

(*Suddenly:*) I'm not fucking staying here!

Scene Sixteen

The squat as before. SHONA, *still drugged up, enters quickly. She's very high, wears someone else's clothes. Sings: (perhaps 'America . . . A-mer-ric-a' from West Side Story) as she changes into her own clothes, throwing off the others, wheeling around in delight.* HARRY *comes in quickly.*

HARRY: Shona — I heard you coming in.

Seeing him she makes a double effort to pretend there's nothing unusual about her being here like this. But her succession of quick smiles conceals her terror.

SHONA: Hello! How are you?

HARRY: How did you get here?

SHONA: Bus. Well, how are you? Nice to see you.

HARRY: Shona —

SHONA: Cup of tea?

HARRY: You discharged yourself.

SHONA: I'm fine.

HARRY: Did they say it was okay?

SHONA: Have the treatment and it'll be all right, they said.

HARRY: You just left didn't you?

SHONA: I can go if you want.

HARRY: Did you, Shona?

SHONA: I don't need to be there.

HARRY: You left.

SHONA: They said I was all right, Harry.

HARRY: Shona, I just have to know for Christ's sake.

SHONA: Don't get rattled Harry. They can't keep me there for ever you know. Think they can. I'm a human being. Not a monkey.

HARRY: What do you want to do?

SHONA: What?

HARRY: I mean, you're going to stay here?

SHONA: Think I should go back, do you?

HARRY: Do you feel okay to stay here?

SHONA: Of course. What's the matter with me? Bit shaky. That's the fucking drugs. It'll wear off. Perfectly normal person.

A pause.

What do you want to do? You ask me.

HARRY: What do you mean?

SHONA (*shrugs*): What are you going to do. Rest of your life.

HARRY (*looks*): Christ, Shona. I don't know what I'm doing.

SHONA: Night on the town then? Share out the MacDonalds!

HARRY: You need to rest, Shona.

SHONA: Why? What's wrong with me?

HARRY: Nothing's wrong with you. I just think you're tired. You're so angry underneath everything else.

SHONA: I'm not angry. Perfectly calm.

HARRY: If I'm helping you, we have to sort it out, that's all.

SHONA: What? Sort out what?

HARRY: Oh, I don't know. I think I'm losing my mind here to be honest. I mean, it doesn't seem real — this — the contact between us. I don't know. I just feel — scared. I want to help you. I don't know how.

SHONA: What help do I need? Anyway it's only the sick who don't know they're sick, you know. If you're scared you must be all right.

HARRY: But you're not.

A pause.

All right. What shall we do?

SHONA: Game of cards?

HARRY: Look, I mean — how do you want to be here.

SHONA: Same as everyone else. Normal being aren't I?

HARRY: Why are you so defensive, Shona?

SHONA: I'm not defensive.

HARRY: Shona, we're not making sense.

SHONA: Think I should go back to the hospital, do you? I'm perfectly all right, Harry. As much right to be here as you have. Only a squat. Not making sense. I'm making sense. Being perfectly rational. Asked you if you wanted a game of cards. Don't know what you mean, no sense. Is there something wrong? What's wrong? Nothing wrong is there? You are not feeling well —

HARRY (*sudden explosion*): Stop fucking around, Shona! (*Slow.*) We have to get through this. We have to try. Or you will end back in the bin.

But his assault has switched her. She's introverted, hiding her terror.

SHONA: All right. If you say so. I'll go back. If that's what you think. I'll go back.

HARRY: Shona, sit down. Please. Look, you need help.

SHONA: All right. I'll go back. Say when.

HARRY: I want to help. I don't know how.

A pause.

SHONA: I could just stay here couldn't I? Wouldn't interfere with you. Don't have to help me.

A pause.

Make you a cup of tea . . . ?

A pause.

Thought I could write for some jobs. Know any jobs going? Anything really. I'm not fussy.

HARRY: I don't know if you're well enough to work.

SHONA: There's nothing wrong. Sound like all the others. Make tea perfectly well, can't I?

HARRY: What'll they do at the hospital when they've discovered you've left?

SHONA: Take it out on someone else, I suppose. I don't know. I don't care.

HARRY: You only had to stay until the end of the month.

SHONA: Changed your tune, haven't you? Stay till the end of the month. Then another month, then a year, two years, then another two years.

A pause.

SHONA: I don't have to stay here, if you don't want. You've got someone coming round, I can disappear.

HARRY: Shona, come on . . .

SHONA: Don't want to be a burden on anyone. Interfere in their lives. It's not right. All got past lives, haven't we? Can't just throw up everything. Don't expect you to.

HARRY: What are you trying to say, Shona?

SHONA: Nothing.

HARRY: I mean if you have something to say, say it.

SHONA: Nothing to say. Just don't want to interfere with your life at all, that's all. What you do's your business — what you've done. It's your past.

HARRY: Look — I was up to my neck in something and I left it and that's it.

SHONA: Easy as that.

HARRY: Why are you trying to provoke me?

SHONA: Feel provoked, do you?

HARRY: You are trying to provoke me.

SHONA: I'm behaving perfectly normally. Made you a cup of tea.

A pause.

HARRY: This can't go on, Shona.

SHONA: Going back on your word, are you? Thought we talked about really being together — our own mad world where it was exciting. America.

HARRY: Yes, but it's not going to work like this, is it?

SHONA: Need something normal do you? Wife, family, nine to five job perhaps.

HARRY: Shona, if you have anything to say, say it. This can't go on.

SHONA (*sudden explosion — as she slings tea in the air*): Then why don't you get out! Get out of my sight! You make me sick! Sick!

HARRY (*slapping her hard*): Stop it! That's enough!

She retreats immediately to the wall. Long pause as she stands there like a hurt, distrusting animal. HARRY sighs. She starts sliding slowly down the wall, simply sits on the floor.

Okay, I'm sorry. Shona, will you get up? Come on, get up will you.

But she's not going to move. He turns away.

Oh, fuck it.

Scene Seventeen

SHONA *lies in much the same position as before, but now has a blanket draped round her on the floor.* HARRY *enters in a change of shirt. It's obvious he's long ago accepted this situation of her being on the floor.*

HARRY (*with salad bowl and plates*): Here, I've made some salad . . . Come on, Shona. You haven't eaten in two days since you came here. Why don't you eat? Didn't even eat the bloody MacDonalds I brought for you.

He gives up coaxing her, leaves her plate by her side, moves to sit away from her, eating his own salad from the bowl. There's just a trace of a feeling here now of two mad people together.

You don't speak to me soon, I won't speak to you. Bark at you. Develop a language of grunts and signs.

Chews. Swallows. But then he has no more appetite for it.

Look, Shona, the others here want me to take you back. I mean, they don't think it's doing you any good — sure, they want to help — they think letting you stay here like this they're doing you a disservice. I mean, I'm fighting them. It'll work, I say, give it time. But two fucking days like this. What am I supposed to do? I just don't know where you are. Yesterday you said one word. 'No.' Two days and you haven't opened your mouth. I'm sorry I hit you. Christ. People get angry. That's it.

Pause.

I mean, I just don't know if you're seeing me now. I don't know where you are, what you're experiencing. I'm even afraid to turn my back on you. I didn't sleep last night for fear you'd stab me to death or something.

Pause.

What does someone have to do to show they care.

Pause.

Look, Shona, what can I do? I can't let you go on lying there, right? Okay, maybe you're not ill, but it's not fucking normal to spend forty-eight hours lying on the floor and not speaking. I haven't seen you move once. I don't know how come you haven't been to the bloody toilet, unless you went in the middle of the night.

Pause.

I'm sorry I hit you, okay. Jesus, it's like living with a dog or pet animal, it is, living with you. I feel guilty, okay? Is that what you want to hear? I do. Now will you please speak to me?

Pause.

So I'm sorry you saw the stupid, fucking photographs before I could tell you. Was that it? I didn't say I wasn't married. You should have trusted. I wanted it to work. It was something I had to trust. I mean, that it would happen, that it was possible — anything was possible. It wasn't stagnant. This   it's no good Shona. It's no life — for you. You know you could be getting something out of life. Ordinary things, movies, whatever.

Pause. He's moving to the end of his tether.

You have to speak to me. You have to make that effort. You have to trust something good will come out of it. That's all you've got, Shona. It's all any of us have — you have to have trust now. Like there's nothing else anymore. Do you hear me? Are you understanding me?

Pause.

If you don't speak to me, Shona, if you don't speak to me in five minutes, I'm going to take you back. I mean it, Shona.

Rises. Turns his back on her.

I really mean it. I don't know what else I can do.

A pause. Then water starts to seep through SHONA's *clothing — pools silently across the floor.*

HARRY (*turning back*): Oh, God, you're pissing yourself.

Scene Eighteen

DR IAN WALL, *at a lectern, giving the last part of his Leeds University conference lecture.*

DR WALL: And so to turn, gentlemen, having taken our look at the various operations available — to our case studies. Our referrals of course are a result of a highly selective procedure, and if we may take a first study to

illustrate — we shall call her Emily — an extreme case warranting extreme treatment and finally, after reaching the very depths of despair and depression, as you will see, referred by myself for psychosurgery at the Brook.

Scene Nineteen

HARRY *in the squat, standing between* SHONA's *two carrier bags, which he's already partly filled with her clothes and gear. He's looking around, a bit 'sadly', for what he's missed. He spots a slim book, drops it in the carrier. And that's it. Except for the picture of the pope he suddenly spots. He moves over to this, pauses. Slowly nods his head, like he knows it's all the Pope's fault. Sighs because he thinks he might like to throw the picture away altogether. But finally has to drop it in one of the two carriers (which will be returned to* SHONA), *lifts both carriers and goes off.*

Scene Twenty

SHONA *in the bin.*

SHONA: It was a bit frightening really — the operation. But I did think it would do some good. They explained it all and everything. Trouble was I just felt terrible for the next year. Dead-like really. Then I was much better — I really was. About six months. Then, I don't know, I don't know why, I just started smashing up the hospital. I mean, I honestly don't know why. Anyway I was sent here. Same as all the others of course. Put me on drugs again. Suppose it's all right. I mean, I'm working, I am — dressing and feeding the ones that can't do it themselves. Get £5 a week. I mean, they're good to me. You can't go on, can't go on smashing up places, can you? You have to, have to fit in with

the rest, don't you? Can't change
everything for you, just because you're
ill. Well, don't suppose I know what
I'm saying really. It's only life after all.

*As the lights dim to put her in
silhouette:*

SPEAKER'S VOICE: Order, order,
order . . .

MEMBER'S VOICE: Will the Secretary of
State for Social Services list in the
official report, how many ECT and
psychosurgery operations took place
on compulsory and voluntary patients,
respectively, in NHS hospitals, in each
of the years between 1975 and 1981?

LUNCH GIRLS

Characters

VEE
BEE
DEE
JAY

Vee, Bee, Dee and Jay are old friends. Now they try to keep in touch by arranging (or trying to arrange) a lunch from time to time.
It doesn't always work out.
Vee is slightly older than the rest – a motherly type, though she has no children.
Jay sounds plump and breathless – she's a dreamer, a little bit lost.
Dee's a bitch, but things really haven't gone her way. The others don't mind her – they think she's beautiful.
Bee's organised, efficient – but not quite as on top of things as she'd have you believe.
The characters in this play are fictitious, but my intention is to give a realistic idea of the way in which a group of middle class ladies speak to each other and of their problems and concerns. They don't have professions or jobs anymore and they are gradually being enclosed in the claustrophobia and isolation of domestic life. Their husbands make no appearance in the action and they come out of the dialogue as rather shadowy, background figures, gradually slipping away. What my ladies project is an increasing awareness of disappointment and disenchantment with men.
To emphasise the isolation of the characters I've written the dialogue in segments and each segment represents a conversation change or a new piece of action. The feeling I would like to achieve is that of the ladies speaking 'out' to the audience as much as to each other, almost as though the audience were on the other side of the conversation. The conversations are sometimes one-way sometimes two-way; we catch one on the 'phone to another, or having tea with another, or saying goodbye at the door to another; we never have all the ladies together although this is what they're planning.
The action takes place in the different rooms of the characters' homes, and the set should *suggest* the hall, bedroom, living-room, kitchen etc. There will need to be subtle changes in lighting, set decor etc. that will reflect the different character then in play, and each conversation segment has a music or sound effects link. The effects are very important to the pace of this play. The feeling, I think, should be chaotic and somewhat hysterical as the characters move, very fast, from one segment of action and dialogue to another, quickly switching their expressions, hats, clothes (and attitudes) as they do so.

R.H.

1

JAY: Hello Bee. Look, I've got to cancel the lunch on Thursday, Joseph's teeth brace has slipped and I've got to take him to the orthodontist. I'm okay for Wednesday.

2

BEE: Sorry Dee, Thursday's off. Jay's Joseph's teeth brace has come apart. He's got bits of metal curled around the upper left incisor. She's okay for Wednesday, so am I.

3

DEE: Bee phoned. She's okay for Wednesday, so is Jay. But unfortunately I can't do it now. I would have been able to but you remember my cleaning lady, Mrs Tebbitt, well she's left to go to live with her son in Yorkshire and I'm interviewing a new one on Wednesday morning, at least I hope I am. I'd have made it on Thursday if we hadn't arranged the lunch.

4

BEE: Are you there Dee?

5

DEE: Well if Jay can't manage Thursday and I can't manage Wednesday, how about Tuesday?

6

VEE: Can't be sure about Tuesday. Harry's mother's chair's blown a fuse. I think she was speeding. She won't be able to get to the Day Centre on her own.

7

BEE: I don't think we're ever going to arrange this lunch.

8

DEE: It's so complicated.

9

JAY: We've all so many things to do.

10

VEE: If you can't manage Wednesday and I can't manage Tuesday and Jay can't manage Thursday, well that leaves Monday or Friday.

DEE: Oh no, I can't manage Friday, Roger's coming back from Saudi Arabia. Monday okay?

VEE: Well, I'll see Bee and Jay at the No No No to the Orbital meeting. I'll speak to them then. But what about Kay?

We hear the continuous sound of the phone bell ringing but it isn't picked up. We hear the sound of a chair being pushed back, table banged, moments of uncertainty etc. and a glass crashes to the ground.

11

BEE: I've tried to phone Kay — she must be out. If she's in she just doesn't answer.

12

JAY: Sorry to hear about Harry's mother. Did she hurt herself?

VEE: Not her. The old bitch — she's fireproof. It's going to take weeks to get the chair mended. In the meantime I can't get her in or out of the car so I've got to walk her to the Day Centre.

JAY: Poor old soul.

VEE: Poor old soul. It's me that's exhausted! Harry won't help. Just flaps his hands and blinks behind his glasses. The ambulance centre are hopeless — they say don't call us we'll call you.

13

JAY: I've been rather hoping you'd ring. About the lunch. Vee's not sure. Harry's mother's set her chair on fire. (*Pause.*) Are you still there?

DEE: I'm still here.

JAY: You sound preoccupied.

DEE: I am preoccupied.

JAY: No one's heard from Kay – she hasn't been seen for weeks. I've tried to phone her. Bee's tried several times. Do you know if Tennyson's back?

DEE: Why should I know if Tennyson's back?

JAY: I'm sorry.

14
BEE: Last I heard he'd been on a course for management skills.

DEE: It's more than management skills he needs with Kay.

15
The phone rings again. There is a vague sound of tinkling glasses etc. The bell changes to ringing tone, the phone is picked up.

16
BEE: Jay's tried and tried. I'm going to try twice more. If she isn't answering, she isn't answering and that's that.

DEE: What about Tennyson? Is he still away?

VEE: Well, Harry says Tennyson's not on the management course. He met somebody who works in Tennyson's department. Nobody's really seen him around. Harry thinks Tennyson doesn't really work anywhere.

17
BEE: Well, John bumped into Tennyson in the tube at Leicester Square. He was obviously in a state. John said that Tennyson looked sort of haunted. Anyway they went off and had a drink in the Salisbury, that's the Victorian pub in St Martin's Lane and they had a real heart to heart.

18
JAY: I had this odd feeling as I drove up to the house – it's strange, Vee, the way Kay keeps her curtains drawn all day. As I drove up I had this weird feeling that the front curtain moved but when I rang the bell there wasn't any answer.

VEE: You should have gone round the back.

JAY: Well, I didn't like to, I thought Kay's entitled to her privacy like everybody else. She knows I'm her friend. If she wanted to talk to me she'd have come to the door.

VEE: I'll go round.

19
DEE: I'm totally pissed off with everybody talking about Kay. She's completely self-indulgent. Keeping out of touch is just her way of being noticed.

BEE: I'm not clever enough to understand that.

20
BEE: Well they've both had the tests. You know first of all they took it for granted it was Kay and so they had tests with the gynaecologist and then the behaviourists and then the psychologist. She'd had every clinical test in the works and they kept on saying to her, 'Oh, there's nothing wrong, it's just that you worry about it and it'll happen in it's time' and all that sort of thing. But all the time it wasn't her, it was him.

JAY: Tennyson?

BEE: Yes. John met this staff welfare chap from Tennyson's department and Tennyson told him and he told John.

JAY: He shouldn't really talk about it.

BEE: Oh it was in absolute confidence! They've made this discovery; nothing to do with ovulation or fallopian tubes or anything like that. They found some men produce spermatoza at a higher temperature than others, so when it enters the womb it kills off all the living organisms.

JAY: First time I've heard of that.

BEE: There's thousands. Much more prevalent than you think.

JAY: Never heard of that.

BEE: He doesn't look as if he's got hot sperm, does he? Not Tennyson?

21

JAY: Terribly sorry, Vee. Just discovered I can't manage Monday after all. Peter's headmaster phoned. They've discovered why it is that when he writes he slopes his loops backwards.

VEE: Oh has he got sloping loops?

JAY: Yes, they've discovered that he really ought to be left handed instead of right handed. They only found out through the sloping loops and all the time they've been putting pressure on him to do his writing with the wrong hand. The head thinks that that explains his bad reading.

VEE: I don't quite see what it's got to do with reading.

JAY: Well that's what they say.

22

BEE: Poppy's a bad reader too — she's terribly slow. She got knocked off her pony the other day. There was a sign that said mind your head but by the time she'd read it it was too late and Muffin had trotted on.

JAY: Sorry about Monday, Friday is my best day. We'll have to leave it till next week.

BEE: Friday's fine. Look I'll be seeing Vee and Dee at the Bring Back the Bridleways meeting, shall I tell them?

23

JAY: There's so much to do. Has anybody seen Kay?

24

VEE: I'm so worried about Kay.

25

BEE: I really am worried about Kay.

26

JAY: I don't know what we're going to do about Kay.

27

DEE: Sod Kay.

Pause.

28

BEE: She's never been so out of touch before. Did you hear about the spermatoza test?

DEE: I heard.

29

JAY: It's a very strange word.

VEE: Strange world?

JAY: No word. Spermatoza — it sounds like an Italian philosopher.

30

BEE: It sounds rather off putting. You know what he has to do? Honestly, well, half an hour before, you know, she wants to conceive, well Tennyson has to sit with his scrotum dangling in a bowl of ice water.

VEE: I suppose it isn't funny.

BEE: No honestly. He had to tell this staff welfare chap because he had to be away for all the tests. This chap told John. Anyway he has to sit like that for at least half an hour so that the sperm gets colder and colder and then he jumps up rushes over to Kay and Bang, Bang.

VEE: It's very sad.

BEE: It's absolutely true.

VEE: Poor Kay.

BEE: Poor Tennyson.

31

BEE: No, Jay can't manage Thursday because she's taking Joseph to the orthodontist and I can't manage Tuesday because I'm taking Peter to the educational psychologist about his slopey backward writing. It's all the wrong way round.

VEE: I think that's the trouble with Tennyson.

32

BEE: Well, if Tom had to sit with his scrotum dangling in a bowl of water he'd go raving mad. Hot or cold.

33

JAY: Kay doesn't seem to be at home.

BEE: I think I'll pop round there tonight.

34

JAY: I spoke to Dee and I saw Vee at the Hands off our Heritage meeting. It seems like the only day now is going to be Wednesday but not this Wednesday, Wednesday next.

DEE: Thank God we're not relying on this lunch. We'd die of malnutrition.

35

VEE: Oh that's fine because Harry doesn't come home on Wednesday evening and they're taking his mother in for assessment in the morning. She'll be in till the weekend, thank God. I'll leave Mata Hari in the garden if the weather's fine otherwise I'll pop her round to Jay and she can spend the day in their basement with Stromboli. I can't leave her wandering around the house. Well, Harry's allergic.

BEE: I don't know what it is about siamese. They make me feel weird.

36

BEE: I phoned Dee and she's okay and that Wednesday's fine for me. It wouldn't be normally because Deirdre comes home early to have her piano lessons with Mrs Amanjaroo, Yes, Mrs Amanjaroo. She's Indian but she's very good. Deirdre calls her Killer Manjaroo but she pushed her through Grade Three with flying colours. Not a merit but at least she passed which for Deirdre is a miracle. She got on the ear like an organ grinder's monkey. Anyway it's all right this Wednesday because Mrs Amanjaroo's daughter's husband is flying back to India to bring back his old mother whose been waiting for an exit visa for nine years. Well I suppose she'll stay on after that and they'll appeal to the Home Secretary – you know – they all do – anyway all the family has to go to London Airport to see them get on the plane. That's what they do, hundreds of them so she's got to go as well. Anyway that's why Deirdre's not having a music lesson.

VEE: Oh that's good. By the way, sorry I couldn't get to the No Way to the Motorway meeting, was everybody there?

BEE: Oh yes, hundreds. Well not hundreds but dozens. We passed a resolution condemning motorway constructions through areas of essential residential potential and it's all off to the minister.

BEE: Well you have to try.

37

VEE: The trouble is they'll give her cat food.

BEE: Harry's mother?

VEE: Oh no she wouldn't care. Mata Hari, she only eats fresh meat otherwise she gets ulcers round her mouth and hairs fall out. Actually it reminds me of Harry's mother. The doctor says it's her diet, she only drinks beer and eats biscuits.

BEE: What Mata Hari?

VEE: No Harry's mother, they inject her with everything else.

38

JAY: I'll just try Kay again.

39

DEE: I don't know why we bother.

VEE: We have to try. If I see the curtain move I'll yell out 'Open up you drunken bitch' through the letterbox. Maybe that'll move her.

DEE: Well I don't know why we bother.

40

VEE: I can understand Kay getting depressed, but I don't know why everyone gets so uptight. Whenever Harry's kids from his first marriage come round I'm quite pleased that we haven't any, I mean that we couldn't . . . if I had kids and they turned out like that.

41

JAY: Dee, is that you?

DEE: Well, of course it's me.

JAY: You sound a bit miffed. Are you sure?

DEE: Miffed? Well, of course I'm sure. I wish you wouldn't use those girly boarding school expressions, Jay.

JAY: I'm sorry. Can I come round?

DEE: No.

JAY: Please.

DEE: No Jay. I said No.

Long pause.

42

JAY: Have you heard about the lunch?

DEE: Oh no, not the lunch.

JAY: It's off again. Bee can't manage Tuesday because of Deirdre's loops and Vee can't manage Wednesday because they're not taking Harry's mother in for assessment after all.

DEE: It's a bloody farce.

43

JAY: I couldn't get through to Dee. Couldn't get through at all. I mean I am her friend, but I couldn't even get her to talk to me.

BEE: I think if there's any more changes we'll call the whole thing off.

44

JAY: Bee says we ought to call the whole thing off, but I do so enjoy our lunches.

DEE: Our lunches, don't be bloody soft, Jay. We've only managed to have three lunches in all the times we've known each other. Someone's kids are always going to the dentist or there's meetings at some bloody school, or someone's horse is sick or dead or running in a race or gone off her head or something.

JAY: Oh don't be beastly, Dee. It's so difficult for some of us. I've got the children and so has Bee, she finds it very difficult, and Vee's got Harry's mother.

45

DEE: I'm fed up with hearing about orthodontists and schools and assessment centres and ponies and music lessons. There's got to be something else.

46

BEE: Yes, I spoke to Dee as well — Dee's a bitch.

47

JAY: Poor old Roger.

VEE: Oh, have you heard something?

JAY: Bee knows.

BEE: Jay wouldn't tell me anything — you know how loyal she is to Dee. If she does know anything she's not letting on, at least not yet. Anyway you know what Jay's like all spiffing and Mums the Word and jolly hockey sticks and all that sort of thing. By the time you've got through the wine gums and the schools and Joseph and Ben and Jason and Peter and John this and John that — it's too exhausting, I don't know how John puts up with it.

Slight pause.

VEE: Well he doesn't, does he? Didn't you know?

BEE: Doesn't what?

VEE: Put up with it, didn't you know?

BEE: Know what? Oh, Vee I wish you wouldn't be so exasperating.

VEE: Well, John inferred to Harry that he's got a girl. Someone who works at the Beeb. Didn't you know?

BEE (*exasperated*): For crying out loud I wish you'd stop saying 'didn't you know'. If I knew I'd say I knew and I wouldn't be asking questions, would I? Well out with it, Vee, if you're going to tell me then tell me, don't keep it to yourself.

VEE (*slight pause*): I'm going to ignore that for the sake of our friendship Bee. I'm not going to take any notice. I'm not going to have a row with you over Jay.

Pause.

Are you still there?

BEE: I'm sorry, Vee. I'll see you Friday.

48
BEE: Apparently he's got this girl in the newsroom at the Beeb. A girl with a great deep voice as far as I can gather. I mean that's probably what John likes about her. I mean she's surrounded him with babies and schools and dentists and measles and mumps. He hides away in his studio all day — I don't think he cares about her. It's her own silly fault.

49
BEE: Jay, how are you darling? How are you feeling? Are you all right?

JAY: I'm fine, Bee.

BEE: Everything okay?

JAY: Everything's fine, Bee.

BEE: Anything I can help?

JAY: Look Bee, if you want to say something please say it. Is there anything you want to say?

BEE: Oh no, no, no, Jay. Did you get hold of Kay?

JAY: No, I didn't get hold of Kay. Did you get hold of Kay? To tell you the truth I couldn't care less about Kay at this moment. I think just for a moment I don't want to think about Kay.

Pause.

BEE: What's wrong Jay?

JAY: You know perfectly well. What's wrong, Jay? One of those other bitches has told you what's wrong, Jay, but they don't know what's wrong, Jay. They don't know (*Slight pause, crying.*)

BEE: I'm sorry Jay.

JAY: I'm so — so unhappy.

BEE: I'm sorry, Jay.

JAY: I'm so unhappy I don't know what to do.

BEE: Is it about John?

JAY: No it's not about John, it's not about John, you don't understand, it's not about John.

50
BEE: She's truly suffering.

VEE: But she won't let me help her.

51
VEE: I can understand that she doesn't want all the tittle tattle but she knows

that I don't tittle tattle, but she thinks everybody's going to tittle tattle about —

DEE: If you say tittle tattle again, I'll slam the phone down.

VEE: Sorry.

52
BEE: Dee, I phoned about the lunch.

DEE: You're not going to tell me about Jay and John are you Bee, you're not are you?

BEE: Vee said you were in a lousy mood.

DEE: Vee's got a mind like an incinerator.

53
VEE: It's so strange we don't seem to be getting along together the way we used to, we're suddenly all at odds with each other.

54
JAY: Dee you've just got to let me come round to talk to you. Just talk to you.

DEE: No, Jay.

JAY: I'm so worried about you.

DEE: I don't want you to be worried about me.

JAY: At least tell me what's wrong. Tell me what I've done.

DEE: No, Jay. It isn't anything to do with you.

JAY: My head's buzzing. I don't understand. Vee and Bee are chat, chat, chatting to each other about John and me. He can have a thousand women as far as I'm concerned. (*Pause*.) Are you still there?

DEE: Yes.

JAY: Listen, I have to talk to you.

DEE: You can't come round, not now, not any more. (*Slight pause*.) I'm sorry.

JAY: Sorry.

DEE: For Pete's sake, Jay. Don't you understand. It's all over. Don't you understand. I'm pregnant.

JAY: You, pregnant?

DEE: Up the spout. Bun in the oven. Family way. What else do you want me to say.

JAY: Oh Dee.

DEE: Oh before you say anything, yes Roger's been away four months and I'm only three months gone. Not that he'll care.

JAY: Oh Dee why didn't you tell me?

DEE: Why should I tell you, Jay? It's nothing to do with you, Jay. Nothing.

JAY: You'll make an appalling mother, Dee. You don't care enough about anyone.

DEE: Well I care about this because that's the hilarious, stupid, ridiculous thing. I want the bloody little brat. I want him.

JAY (*sobbing*): Oh Dee, Dee.

DEE: Well, why shouldn't I. You've got your Ben and your Toby and your Jason and your Joe. I'm always hearing about their teeth and their illnesses and their ponies and their schools. You never stop talking about them.

Pause.

JAY: Oh, all those times we've been together, I thought . . . I thought we were lovers.

DEE (*snorting*): Lovers, don't make me laugh.

Pause, JAY sobs.

I'm sorry Jay, I don't want to hurt you. You're so possessive.

JAY: Who is it?

DEE: That's what's so funny. He told me it was so safe.

JAY: Who?

DEE: It's Tennyson.

JAY: Oh Dee, how could you – that's so unfair.

DEE: Not hockey? You piss me off, Jay.

Pause.

JAY: You greedy bitch.

DEE: Naughty, naughty.

JAY: Took me from John and now you're taking Tennyson from Kay.

DEE: I didn't take anyone from anyone. You both came willingly – Tennyson wanted to escape his frigid wife and you were getting away from your frigid self.

Pause.

JAY: Why are you so willing to hurt me.

DEE: I've had enough of you, Jay. I'm fed up with your humility and your whining and your incessant talk of kids. You didn't want an affair with me, you wanted us to be girl scouts together. I need some passion in my life, Jay, I wasn't looking for domestic bliss.

JAY: I'm so sorry.

DEE: Yes . . . I'm sorry too.

Pause.

JAY: I'm no good to anyone – the kids don't care for me.

DEE: Oh, for Christ's sake.

JAY: I dash round, looking after them all, and sometimes I see five pairs of eyes looking up at me from the table . . . not thinking about me but with . . . curiosity. A sort of wonder who I am, and why I'm there.

DEE: I shouldn't get too paranoid about it Jay.

Pause.

JAY: What about Tennyson?

DEE: Tennyson? He came, if you'll pardon the expression, and went. He dinged my bell and now he's gone and I think we helped each other. I've no

particular wish to see him again.

Pause.

JAY: I love you, Dee.

DEE: You're going to have to stop saying that.

Pause.

JAY (*brightly*): Will you be there Friday?

DEE: Friday?

JAY: The lunch.

DEE: The lunch. The stupid lunch. It's bizarre. Ha. Ha. Ha.

JAY: It isn't funny.

DEE: It's funny all right.

JAY: Please.

DEE: Yes, I'll be there. I'll be there.

55

BEE: I'm so looking forward to Friday.

VEE: I just need to get away from this house.

BEE: Harry's mother?

VEE: No, it's Harry. Haven't you heard, he's been made redundant.

BEE: Redundant. After all those years. Wasn't he on defence work?

VEE: Yes, that's the trouble. It was all so top secret. Harry used to prepare assessments and reports every month on Soviet Economic Planning and he'd send it out to the DS of SPD or some such title at the Foreign Office and then this chap would read it and write some comments and send it back to Harry who was the IIC of P or something. They suddenly discovered that this DS of SPD should have been sending the reports onto another department to somebody called the DG of FMP.

BEE: It sounds very confused.

VEE: Well, it is. You see, over the years Harry's been getting these things back and he's always thought they've been copied and sent on somewhere else. Now he's found that they've just gone round in a circle. Nobody had ever seen his reports.

BEE: That's ridiculous.

VEE: Yes, that's how Harry feels.

BEE: But doesn't that other chap, the DG of FMP still need Harry's reports?

VEE: No, he died years ago and they didn't replace him. That's what's really happened. Harry's dreadfully upset — he feels he's wasted his life. He almost resigned on the spot, but they told him not to be so silly and they made him redundant instead.

BEE: Poor Harry, he must be devastated.

VEE: Perhaps it's all for the best. I don't know if you've ever seen any of Harry's reports, but they're terribly pompous and confused and absolutely full of aggression. I mean if they'd ever arrived in the right place, he'd have probably caused a world war or something.

56
JAY: I've just had the oddest visit from Harry. He's become a wig salesman.

BEE: A wig salesman?

JAY: Yes, I never even knew he was a baldy but he is. He's got this job and they send him out on training and so he came round yesterday to demonstrate to John. You know what Harry's like, he's a bit slow and fumbly and he's supposed to give this big chat and we all practically fell asleep by the time he got to the point. Anyway, he gives this big sales pitch and then suddenly he lifts off his wig and you see that he is as bald as a brass monkey underneath.

BEE: I didn't know that John was bald.

JAY: No, John isn't. It's Harry, he was just trying it out to see if he can get his sales pitch right, he was practising. He just wanted John to listen to him.

BEE: See you Friday, Jay.

57
DEE: Oh Vee, you're not going to tell me about Harry as well.

VEE: Has someone told you?

DEE: Everybody's told me. They can't talk about anything else.

VEE: Actually I'm so pleased he's taking it so well.

DEE: What the wig job?

VEE: No, the redundancy. He's quite pleased with the job, and it's lucky he's bald really, otherwise I don't know what he'd do. Actually to see him do the hairpiece demonstration makes me realise how very much like his mother Harry is. I mean she's nearly bald and she's got the same great domey sort of head. It's natural really — he must have got it from somewhere. He ought to take her out on demonstrations and she could sit there cackling in her chair and then, when the moment strikes, he could whip off both their hair pieces together. Be sensational. Some of the salesmen make a £1,000 a week.

58
BEE: I can't get used to Harry. It's schizoid. It's like a party trick — one minute you see him with his wig on and the next he's bald as a billiard ball.

JAY: John says it's a sort of way of exposing himself — a wish for self-destruction. He's sort of 'come out' as a bald person after all these years because he's so ashamed of being made redundant. He wants to show his humiliation.

BEE: Poor old Harry.

59
JAY: Harry doesn't seem to mind so much anymore.

BEE: Tom's firm's reducing as well.

JAY: I was surprised to hear about Tom's firm. I thought they were doing so well.

BEE: Oh the firm's doing a bomb, but you know they were one of the first to go computerised, so they had roomfuls of these huge machines with hundreds of people buzzing away at them. Tom loved it and quite suddenly they cleared them all out and they've got this one machine that does all the work the others did.

JAY: I suppose it's progress.

BEE: It even sends monthly reports to itself but the hilarious thing is it churns out so much paper and they've sacked so many people, there's nobody to read the reports.

JAY: But, John, isn't he worried about it?

BEE: Oh no, he's dealing with catering accounts and so when things get a bit edgy he transfers part of the budget from the staff canteen and adds it to the cost of the directors' dining room. Of course they're delighted because they see the cost of staff welfare going down and so they think he's doing a marvellous job. The way it shows now, if you worked it out then it seems like they're spending eighty quid a day on each director's lunch. They'd be too embarrassed to sack him.

JAY (*laughing*).

BEE: Anyway they've given him a rise and a bonus and we're all going to Majorca for Easter. Any moment now he'll be on the main board.

60
DEE: You're not going to tell me about Harry's wig job?

BEE: You've heard.

DEE: Yes, and I also know you're going to Majorca for your holiday.

BEE: News travels fast.

61
JAY: Is Friday still okay?

DEE: I think so but I might have to leave early because there's an American film director who's doing the remake of *Fanny By Gaslight* – this time with *music*. I'm doing the sociological research.

JAY: Sociological research?

DEE: Oh, the bits about the fallen women and all that sort of thing. They're going to spend a fortune. All it means is that I've got to sit in the British Museum having my bum pinched by Freud and Bertrand Russell and all that sort of thing.

62
JAY: They chose the right one.

VEE: Well it'll keep her off the streets.

JAY: Have you heard about that as well?

VEE: I was joking. (*Pause.*) Is there something?

JAY: Well, Bee says that Kay told her that Roger's supposed to have seen her once in the Café Royal with two Arabs and a bloke from British Leyland. Kay said she was working for an escort service.

VEE: Dee's just the right type for a high-class tart.

JAY: High-class? Anyway it all ended with her throwing a glass of brandy over Roger and he tearing her dress. The funny thing was he was supposed to be with two women himself – one from *British Celonese* and the other from *American Vogue*. He said it was on business.

VEE: Well he does travel in ladies underwear.

Laughter.

63
BEE: Sorry, Vee, now it's Dee can't manage Friday. She's very sorry but she's suddenly got this temporary job with a film producer who calls her out all hours of the day and night.

VEE: Jay still can't manage Mondays because of Peter's loops and I've still got problems with Harry's mother every Tuesday.

BEE: Well I'm okay nearly every day next week. Deirdre's finished with the orthodontist and Poppy doesn't have to be taken out of school for riding lessons anymore because their new gym mistress is into horses and takes them all in a whole group. The trouble is you have to pay for a whole term in advance so I'm going to be overdrawn with the payments on Muffin.

VEE: Muffin?

BEE: Yes, we bought him on easy payments. You can do that. Tom calls it horse purchase.

64
JAY: Well I definitely can't manage Wednesdays. I've been trying to get in touch with Dee, have you heard from her.

VEE: I spoke to her this morning.

JAY: She's always out when I call.

65
VEE:Someone ought to try and contact Kay.

66
DEE: Sod Kay.

67
JAY: I'm going to have one last desperate attempt at Kay.

68
VEE: Dee says 'sod Kay'.

69
BEE: No we can't just sod Kay — she's our friend. We've always included her. We can't exclude her when she's in trouble.

JAY: Dee can.

BEE: Oh you know what Dee's like. She doesn't see any further than her own psychological needs. Everybody else can go hang.

JAY (*crying*).

BEE: What's wrong, Jay?

70
BEE: Jay was talking about Dee and suddenly she burst into tears.

71
JAY: Can I come round and talk to you?

BEE: No, it's not convenient now, Jay. Deirdre will be home soon and Poppy's got to be got ready for the Brownies.

Pause.

JAY: Oh, I'm so pleased she's started Brownies.

BEE: Well, she has and she hasn't. She hasn't got the uniform. I thought we'd wait and see how she got on first before we spent the money. She just wears the yellow toggle and the brown shoes. I'm not sure if she's going to like it.

Slightly longer pause.

72
VEE (*urgently — sounding breathless*): Look, I've only got a minute. I have to dash to the hospital. Tell the others would you, Dee? You're the only one I could catch in.

DEE: Who is it?

VEE: It's Vee. Don't you recognise my voice? About the lunch.

DEE: Of course. Sorry Vee. What's the trouble?

VEE: I'm trying to keep my head together. I'm just about managing. I think I'm all right. Look, Harry's had a heart attack. It's only mild but they've taken him to University College. Fortunately, he was just outside when it happened and he got mouth-to-mouth resuscitation from one of the nurses.

73

BEE: Worrying over the redundancy.

JAY: Harry wasn't the type for a wig salesman. Probably took it out of him quite badly doing that. I mean he's a quiet man — it wasn't his sort of job.

BEE: Not for the Harry's of this world. You know you never see him get upset. With Tom he starts to break the furniture.

JAY: Probably better — to have an outlet.

74

DEE: I wish somebody would tell me whether the bloody lunch is on, or whether the bloody lunch is off.

75

JAY: Typical, Dee.

76

VEE: Yes, I'd like to come. I'd like to come. I can't see Harry — he's in intensive care and he's so full of tubes and catheters and sensory pads and all that and they've got him in an oxygen mask so I can't talk to him and he wouldn't hear me if I did. If it's still on I'll just pop out from the bedside and have lunch. It won't harm Harry and it'll certainly help me.

77

BEE: We've all got to come. We'll change it to be near the hospital so that Vee doesn't have to leave Harry for too long. We'll all do it for Vee.

JAY: Oh yes we must, we must do it for Vee. (*Slowly*:) Will Dee be there?

BEE: Yes, even Dee's coming. I do think it's wonderful to do things for your friends.

JAY: It will work out very well. Jason and Peter have got their Founders Day and so they are really off school but they can stay on and have lunch there with the bigger boys after the speeches. It only means I'll have to get the girl in to look after Joseph and John will have to walk Ben down to his clarinet lesson.

78

BEE: Everybody's coming.

79

JAY: I promised Vee I'd look in on Harry's mother. She's making a lot of trouble down at the Day Centre. They can't understand why they've been landed with her every day instead of once a week. I told Vee, if I get the chance I'll take her for a drive maybe and give them a break.

BEE: I think you're the only one who can cope with her, Jay.

JAY: It's the least I can do.

80

DEE: Oh it's you, Jay.

JAY: It's your bad penny, Dee. You can't lose me. I'll always turn up.

DEE: I wasn't trying to lose you. *(Gently.)* I was just trying . . . to tell you *(Pause.)*

JAY: Jay just wanted to talk to Dee . . . Jay just wanted to talk — now that she's not allowed to come and see her Dee.

DEE: Oh for Christ's sake . . . all right.

JAY: Say if you mind. If you mind I'll just ring off.

DEE: It's okay, Jay.

JAY: I don't want to interfere with your life.

DEE: You won't interfere with my life.

JAY: I mustn't be a load on your shoulders.

DEE: It's okay.

JAY: If you think I'm being a burden to you, you just have to say.

DEE: It's all right.

JAY: I can't *help* what I'm doing. I just have —

DEE: For God's sake, Jay — will you say what you're going to say, instead of apologising for saying it.

Pause — JAY sobs.

Oh Jay, I'm sorry. Look, Jay, you know my temper — you've simply got to understand   it's over between you and me. And if the truth was said, then there was never really anything between us.

Pause — JAY sobs more loudly.

Oh for Christ's sake.

JAY (*after a pause — in a wheedling voice*): You said I was your little flower.

DEE: I say a lot of stupid things.

JAY: You let me kiss and fondle you.

DEE: Oh so bloody what?

JAY (*crying*): But I love you, love you Dee. I love you.

DEE: Don't be stupid, Jay.

JAY: I can't help it.

DEE: That isn't my fault. Look you caught me at a funny time — you were just one affair, Jay. I've had dozens — men and women, they're all the same to me. But for Christ's sake Jay, apart from the odd grope we didn't do anything — it was just —

JAY: But I'd have done anything for you.

DEE: Oh no you wouldn't . . . you never even said anything that was real or deep . . . and as for the physical side — I couldn't make head or tail of you, Jay. You were too prim! You're too frightened.

Pause — JAY sighing.

Not really enjoying it.

JAY: You're so cruel to me, Dee, but I don't mind about that. All I want is to be allowed to love you.

DEE: Look Jay — I'm not your old hockey mistress with hot hands and flushed cheeks. That's your world, not mine.

JAY: I don't even mind if you say that. I just want to hear you talk.

DEE: Oh go to hell.

Pause.

JAY: I'll ring off if you want me to.

Pause.

DEE: Just talk about something else.

81
BEE: Dee have you heard about Harry?

DEE: Poor Harry. How old was he — is he?

BEE: 44.

DEE: Only 44, I thought he was *much* older than that.

82
JAY: Poor Harry. He's so good and so kind. He never had a bad word to say for anybody.

DEE: He was always such a . . . quiet man. Vee has been told he'll never *recover*. His brain's impaired.

83
DEE: I suppose he'll go about with one of those sloppy grins on his face for the rest of his life, poor sod. Poor Vee, she'll have them both in *wheelchairs*, Harry and his mother — his first wife must be laughing her head off — I mean he divorced her for Vee, didn't he? Now Vee's been left with the problem. She should never have married him — they could've lived together. She could've packed him off back to the first wife and said 'Look, he's still legally yours so you can look after him.'

84
DEE: You know if he dies Vee won't even get insurance. He signed that

away to cover the maintenance for the first wife. She gets nothing.

JAY: Poor Vee.

85
DEE: Stupid bitch.

86
JAY: I just need to hear you talk.

DEE: Not again for Christ's sake.

JAY: I can't help it.

87
JAY: Bee's heard from Kay.

88
VEE: It was so nice of her to make the effort.

89
BEE: You could hardly call it a conversation — she was just kind of making contact — it hardly sounded like her at all. I felt that she could hardly keep her head together. You know what I mean?

VEE: Oh it's *so* sad. *Poor* Kay.

90
JAY: Bee said it was just like talking to someone who'd been drugged.

DEE: She probably had, it's those suppressive drugs.

91
BEE: It was just like a *drunk* walking down a *straight* line. You could *feel* the concentration. It was as if anything I said to her didn't go in until four or five seconds too late.

VEE: Did she say anything about — herself?

BEE: No, I can't say that she did. Actually I think that she'd told herself that she'd got to phone up about Harry but she couldn't pull herself together enough to phone you. So she phoned me. Anyway towards the end of the conversation

I rather gather that she was going to phone you as well.

VEE: Perhaps we can help each other.

92
JAY: If only she could find her way back to us — her old chums. Well she wouldn't feel so sorry for herself.

BEE: Who Vee?

JAY: No Kay, of course, Kay.

93
BEE: I thought I'd better just tell you.

94
JAY: Dee, did you hear that Kay phoned Bee?

DEE: Oh is *she* back in the land of the living?

JAY: It was really about Harry.

DEE: I suppose something had to get through to that befuddled brain.

JAY: You are a bitch, Dee. You really are a bitch.

DEE: I could've told you that long ago.

95
JAY: Vee, is there any news?

VEE: No, there's no change, not really — they say they have to keep him like that for at least a week — under sedation — so that the tissues mend. They'll gradually let him back when he can cope with things.

JAY: That's good news.

VEE: The consultant says as long as he's rested there's no reason why he can't be home quite soon.

JAY: Oh that is good news.

Slight pause.

VEE: No, it was the way he said it. He didn't say better — he said have him home — and he gave me a queer look as though he didn't know how to speak to me.

JAY: Oh Vee.

VEE: No, I don't think he meant better.

JAY: Oh Vee.

VEE: We were standing at the foot of Harry's bed when he said it to me, me and one of the young nurses, when he came up to us. He's only a young man — he's younger than Harry — to be a consultant I mean — but you know they have a way of looking sort of grey and mature and serious when they talk to you and it makes you think of them as older. He had this clipboard under his arm and his white coat flying open and the stethoscope round his neck. The funny thing was that I was just standing looking at Harry propped up on all the pillows and I kept thinking to myself how terrible Harry looked and then as I thought it I put it out of my mind because it seemed disloyal to be thinking that. They've put a funny woolly sort of night cap on his head to stop him getting cold and you know what a fat face Harry's got, well lying back there with all the pillows and the heavy face and that night cap he looked like something out of one of those awful paintings. And every now and then his eyes open and he gives a quick look round like an alligator, not actually seeing anybody; the eyes dart round and the lids close again and he looked so strange and so senile, almost as though he's dead and though the spirit's gone the body's still living. It's weird, Jay; it's very, very weird — I never expected to think about Harry like that. Anyway I was standing there and strange thoughts kept coming into my mind. I kept on saying to myself 'that's not my Harry, that's not my Harry' — and truly I thought I'd come into the wrong place. I didn't really want anybody to think I was connected with him. Do you think that awful, Jay? And then suddenly this consultant popped up in front of me with his coat flapping like wings and he completely shut Harry off from

my gaze. Do you know the first thought that came into my mind was what a good looking young man he was — the consultant. Why did I think that at that time, Jay? Why *then*. I wondered if I really loved Harry, I've never thought about anybody else before. I've only ever loved Harry. And then when he spoke to me with this sort of false concern in his voice — I know they have to do it — it's their job — but I really hated him. I really began to hate him for being so young and so good looking and so well. (*Pause.*) It was so irrational. I know he was only trying to help Harry. D'you know a terrible fleeting thought came across my mind. I wondered if he fancied me.

96

BEE: The wonderful thing about Vee is that she's so controlled.

Long pause.

97

JAY (*slowly*): We must all try and help Vee. When we meet we must all find a task to do for her like . . .

BEE: Like helping with Harry's mother.

DEE (*sardonically*): Taking back the library books.

98

VEE: It's so good of you all to want to help me but really there's nothing. It's just your friendship I want just now. I'm so looking forward to meeting you all at the lunch.

Long pause.

99

We hear the sound of tyres on gravel, telephone bells mixing with the donging of a church bell. We hear the steady plod of hearse bearers and 'Ashes to ashes', etc. vaguely in the distance, then steady plodding again, tyres on gravel.

Pause.

100

DEE: I *knew* we'd never make that bloody lunch.

BEE: I worked out that Harry must've died just at the moment when we were due to meet.

101

JAY: Poor old Harry.

BEE: Poor old Vee.

102

DEE: I know this is going to sound awful but have you noticed how it *suits* Vee being a widow. She's got that clean, cold, steely-eyed look and the black clothes set the figure off so well for someone who's plump.

BEE: Of course, she always hated Harry's family. The mother was wished on her. I think the kids came round once but you know she had a way of seeing people off when she doesn't want them.

103

VEE: I telephoned three days before the funeral but the wife wouldn't speak to me. I spoke to the boy, the eldest son and he started shouting all sorts of obscenities at me. It was terrible. It seemed to go on for ages but I couldn't put the phone down. I felt I had to listen. I just waited till he finished. In the end he started crying . . . I told him when the funeral was but he said they wouldn't come. I suppose it was for the best.

104

BEE: It was almost as though she expected it . . . prepared for it. To be frank I always felt that she found Harry a bit of an irritation, I mean he'd sit there in the garden in those revolting shorts and with a napkin tucked into his shirt, d'you know what I mean.

105

VEE: Harry wasn't a tidy man. Nothing was ever kept in order. I'd have to tidy everything.

106

JAY (*breathlessly*): D'you know I went to pop down to see Vee with some flowers. The old girl's gone! I saw her being taken off in an ambulance. She was shouting her head off about it being Harry's house, but of course Vee was unmoved.

107

VEE: Of course I had to let his mother go. It was too sad. She reminded me of Harry sitting there and I found I couldn't bear it. You know I realise they had many physical similarities but they were quite unalike. She's a tough old bird. I admired her but Harry was weak, he gave into everything. If he'd been more like her he'd have hung on . . . still they're all the same, aren't they — men?

JAY: They're all weak.

Long pause.

108

DEE: Roger phoned Vee, from Saudi Arabia. He'd only just heard the news. He wanted to pay his respects and I'm sure he'll be writing to you. He was very fond of Harry . . . (*Pause.*) No I don't think he'll be back for some while. He's thinking of staying on out there. It's his sort of life, lots of turbans and violence and young Arab boys.

109

JAY (*spitefully*): Even if he did come back it wouldn't be to Dee. She didn't really understand him. Of course, you know he used to dress up in women's clothes on a Sunday afternoon? Sunday best! Of course with Dee being so perverse she was delighted. Then he started wearing her knickers going to work and that seemed to upset her. She didn't mind him doing it in the house.

VEE: They have it all their own way.

DEE: Roger had it both ways.

110
VEE: Men.

111
BEE: Vee, Tom asked me to phone. He's just got back from Japan and he was so shocked to hear about Harry. He's flaked out otherwise he'd have phoned himself. I can honestly say that he really loved Harry and that's why he wanted to come to the funeral. If he'd known he'd have really got back in time. He'd have tried. (*Pause*.) To be honest we hardly ever see Tom ourselves these days. Ever since that business with the accounts his firm's kept promoting him and promoting him and he's become a sort of trouble-shooter for the main board. Every time there's a problem somewhere they send him off and being Tom he just fiddles around with the figures and tells them everything is all right. I think they know really but they're all in it up to their necks and it's quite convenient to have one of them who just doesn't mind what he puts his signature to, then if anything goes wrong they can blame him and pretend they didn't know anything about it. Of course, Tom's building up a dossier on all of *them* as well, so they won't get away scot free. Anyway a car fetches him in the morning so that he can have breakfast with the chairman and then it brings him back in the evening after they've juggled the accounts. It's after midnight sometimes when he gets back. Now they're sending him to South America on some other giant swindle. When you think its all government money . . . me and the kids won't see

him for ages. Tom knows it's wrong, of course, but he's too weak to say no.

VEE: Weak? Oh yes, bloody men.

112
JAY: John wanted to come to the funeral, he really did Vee. He even phoned me and told me that he wanted to come but the way things are now he has to get planning permission from *her* before he even phones me. He wanted to come out of respect for Harry, but I think he's a bit shame-faced about what he's done. He's trying to pretend it's temporary but I know she'll never let him back, that girl from the Beeb. She's got him wound round her little finger and he just does whatever he's told. She taking him off to the Greek islands now. He's going to become a great artist and find himself! She really just needs somebody to carry her bags. He left a note saying he was going to work things out. Work things out! He couldn't work a clockwork teddybear. He's totally selfish of course.

VEE: Selfish . . . Oh yes, men.

BEE: I think if Tom were given the choice between me and the kids and his work he'd choose . . .

113
JAY: I suppose John was never really *there* at the best of times.

114
DEE: Really, Roger never really liked women. That was his problem, it turned out to be mine as well.

115
VEE: By the way has anybody been in touch with Kay? I was *so* sorry she couldn't come to the funeral. I think I'll pop round. Look we'll arrange the *lunch* and then I'll pop round and see. Perhaps she can come.

BEE: Well *I* can't make it Tuesday because of Speech Day and I know that . . .

116
JAY: As long as we can meet Thursday
    after one then I'm . . .

117
DEE: No, I'm pretty free . . . most of
    the time.

118
VEE: Oh that's *good* then. Let's make it
    Wednesday . . .

Fade.

THE SHELTER

To the memory of my mother,
and for my daughter, Lesley

Characters

ANNIE, *late thirties*
NORA, *late forties*
MARY, *sixty*
PETER, *fourteen*
ROSIE, *thirteen*
BERT, *sixty*
BILLY, *fifty-six*

Time: 1942.
Place: an air-raid shelter in Stepney.

ACT ONE

Darkness.
  Air-raid siren. Soft becoming louder.
The sound of enemy planes. Gun fire.
Search-lights beat across the sky. Cut.
Light.
  The interior of a long brick shelter.
We look down the middle. Exit far rear.
Bunks either side. On the floor are
mattresses with blankets and pillows.
  Three WOMEN, *a* GIRL *and* BOY *of*
about fifteen enter.

ANNIE (*pushing* PETER): Well move
  yourself then! And I told you to leave
  that wireless up-stairs. Don't take a bit
  of notice . . .

PETER: What's wrong with listening to
  the wireless . . . Nothing else to do in
  'ere . . . Only knitting needles,
  whispers and cups to listen to . . .

NORA: That's a fact . . .

ANNIE: The time you un-plug the
  soddin' thing we could all be blown to
  smithereens.

MARY: Music while you work and music
  while you wait. Ain't we lucky . . .?

ANNIE: Where's your old man, Mary?

MARY: Up the Billet half pissed, I
  shouldn't wonder. 'I aint bloody
  going to kip in a shelter', he says. 'If
  your time's up, it's up.' Brave my arse.
  If he wasn't half sloshed you'd be able
  to sell him off as a human vibrator.
  Nerves is shocking. Thought mine was
  bad enough.

ANNIE: Hear that, Nora?

NORA: Ain't they all the same? Two
  pints and they wanna take on the
  German army. Rosie, did you pick up
  the sandwiches?

ROSIE: I thought you had 'em.

NORA: Well I ain't. Silly cow!

ANNIE: It's all right, Nora, we've got
  plenty to go round.

MARY: So have I.

NORA: Ta. Rosie, you take the top bunk
  tonight . . . Let's get settled . . .

ANNIE: Bleedin' life, en it?

MARY: You can say that again. Every
  bloody night this week.

NORA: I was thinking of taking up
  permanent residence. Don't know why
  I pay bleedin' rent. I ain't lived in the
  flats since 1940!

ANNIE: What's horrible about it is the
  waiting. I said to my old man when he
  was home on leave, 'It's all right for
  you. You've got a gun and tank to
  defend yourself with. All we do at
  home is *wait.*' He didn't like that.

MARY: I bet he didn't.

NORA: It's worse waiting . . . Your head
  imagines all sorts of things.

MARY: Yer. And worse than that, you
  never know if you're gonna find your
  home when you do get out.

ANNIE: Broke poor Nellie Ambrose's
  heart didn't it? Come out into the
  light of day, and there was her house,
  flat as a pancake. Lived there fifty
  years. Gone in a minute. Don't bear
  thinking about. I hate this fucking
  war!

PETER: Mum, d'you have to swear . . .
  like that . . .?

MARY: Oooo, listen to her young 'un.
  Annie, is he training for the priesthood
  or something?

NORA: Make a fine priest . . . Still, it's
  a job, en it?

ANNIE: If I have any more of his cheek
  he'd better start training to *run*. Make
  a bloody saint swear the way we're
  living. These youngsters think it's a
  game, I'm sure they do.

NORA: Never mind, love. It'll be over
  one day.

ANNIE: Yer. I suppose so. Does get you
  down at times though, don't it? Still,
  we're lucky to be alive I suppose.
  Although sometimes I think we'd be

better off out of it . . . Never knowing . . .

NORA: At least your two little 'uns are safe.

MARY: And my eldest daughter's girls, thank gawd . . . Although when I think about it, they could have left me the kids – and taken my old man! He's more trouble than ten kids.

ANNIE: I can't stand it, having to go and see 'em and then leaving. Leaving 'em with strangers. Breaks me bleedin' heart. Mind you, she's a lovely woman. Right lar-de-dar, but decent with it. Don't make you feel you're someone just crawled out of the brickwork. You know . . .?

MARY: My Bert's a bit touchy when it comes to those people. Says they scabbed during the general strike. Got a memory like an elephant when it comes to strikes and the workers. (*Pause.*) Quietened down a lot now. Pity in some ways . . . Real leadership qualities he had. Nothing like a useless war to knock the stuffing out of a man.

NORA: Evacuation's a God-send for some. But my Sissie's girl . . . Mind, when the poor little cow told her mother, well naturally Sissie thought she was lying; you know, to get home. 'Course, the wife found the dirty old bastard one night sitting on the poor kid's bed. Child was petrified. Lucky Sissie didn't get him before the police. She'd have castrated him.

ANNIE: It's too horrible to think about. The amount of young girls it happens to . . .

ROSIE: What happened, mum?

NORA: Nose ointment.

PETER: Shall I plug the wireless in?

ANNIE: You and that bloody wireless. Just mind you don't blow all the lights. I don't want to be reading by candlelight again.

MARY: Come on then, let's have a bit of music, cheer us up. You're a long time dead. Get on with it, Pete!

PETER *fixes the socket into the light holder from the top bunk.*

ANNIE: Time that thing warms up it'll be time to leave.

MARY: I'll be glad when I get me letter. Get out of it all.

ANNIE: Don't know what I'd do if I couldn't go down the hop-fields. It's bleedin' hard but I wouldn't miss the break for the world. The smell of the wet hops . . . Nights round the cook-house fire . . . a little sing-song . . . And safe from all this . . . fear and dread.

NORA: This is the first year I've missed fruit picking, d'you know that?

ANNIE: Bleedin' war puts a stop to everything.

MARY: Ha. That's true for most I suppose. But some don't do so bad. That bloody Harry Cutler must be a millionaire by now. How he gets hold of stuff beats me. Nylon stockings he was flogging the other day! Nylon, mind you! Bleedin' rogue he is. Looked fit enough to be called up if you ask me.

ANNIE: He was. But the clever sod joined the fire brigade and then pretended to hurt his back.

NORA: Just like Billy Dod. He joined the police.

MARY: Him! He's the biggest villain walking the streets of Stepney. I'll give my old man his due, he's got bad eyes, but at least he joined the ARP.

ANNIE: Funny he ain't looked in yet . . .

MARY: Yer, well, he'll make sure the pub's safe first, then the rest of the pubs; then he'll see if I'm all right!

NORA: Bless him!

BERT *enters with a big smile on his face.*

Hello, Bert!

MARY: Talk of the devil . . .

BERT (*under the influence*): Good evening, ladies, boys and girls. I've just popped in to tell you that Hitler is giving the Royal Group of Docks a bashing tonight. The sky's lit up, bright as a blast furnace. We can only hope the planes don't get this far. I shouldn't think so myself, seems as how we got treated last night. Well, how's everyone?

MARY: Did you make sure the Billet had it's black-out's up, dear? And by the way, I've left the dog upstairs.

BERT: Left the dog . . .? What, upstairs? What's up with you for Gawd's sake? Supposing she gets bombed? That's the bleedin' latest! Leaving a poor dog on it's own with this racket going on.

MARY: You should have taken her with you. She was sulking. Wouldn't budge. Bleedin' animal; worse than you if it don't get up the pub.

PETER (*still fiddling with the wireless*): Shall I go'n fetch Blackie for you, Mr Walker?

ANNIE: You ain't going nowhere with them planes out there!

BERT: Very nice of you, young Pete, but I've got to do me rounds presently. I'll collect her then. And how's my lovely little Rosie?

ROSIE: Hello, Mr Walker. I'm all right.

BERT (*to* PETER): Wish I was your age, I don't mind telling yer . . . Well then, where's the cocoa? Blimey, d'you feel that one?

MARY: Sit down you silly sod. The only thing wobbling is you. Sit down before you fall down. (*She opens a flask, pours him drink.*) Give us your cups, Annie . . . Nora . . .

NORA: Just what I fancy. Rosie, give us the cups out of the bag.

ROSIE *passes a cup.*

Don't you want a drink?

ROSIE: Don't fancy one yet.

NORA: What's the matter with you?

ROSIE: Just don't fancy cocoa!

BERT: That's the first sign . . .

NORA: What you on about?

BERT: Young Rosie, here. Don't want her cocoa. That's the first sign.

MARY: First sign of what? Leprosy!

BERT: Love! Couldn't drink me beer for days after I met you.

MARY: Stone me. You've made up fer it since. What's the reason for that I wonder . . .

BERT: I bet young Pete there knows something about it . . .

PETER (*embarrassed*): Bleedin' don't . . . Don't know what's up with the wireless tonight . . .

ANNIE: You mess about with it too much. He had the back out of it the other night. Just caught him nicely. He's ruined me best clock. Had it since I was married. Took that to pieces as well. His father'll brain him when he comes home. Bleedin' boy can't stop fiddling about with things. Want's to look inside everything. If he could get inside his own head he would . . .

BERT: Curiosity killed the cat. You heard that one, Pete?

PETER: No . . .

ROSIE: Peter ain't nosey.

BERT: Curious ain't being nosey, yer silly cow.

MARY: All right, Brain of Britain, here's your cocoa. That'll keep your mouth occupied.

BERT: Curiosity means your curious. Are you with me?

PETER: No.

ANNIE: Bert, stop talking to him while he's messing about with that thing.

ROSIE: But Mr Walker, what's curious mean?

BERT: Well, love, curious means . . . you're curious. And that's curiosity, like.

ROSIE (*pause*): Oh . . .

BERT: Don't know what they teach the kids in school these days.

NORA: No doubt about it Bert, you had the benefits of a good education. (*She winks at* MARY:) Right clever old stick you've got there, Mary.

MARY: Oh, dead clever. More dead than clever, mind!

ANNIE: Take no notice of 'em Bert. Are you still driving your motor? Ain't seen it in the street lately. Don't tell us we're going to have to go down hopping on a train.

BERT: It's being overhauled. But don't worry; it'll be ready by September.

MARY: Ain't it time you done your rounds. Bleedin' street might be burning down for all we know.

BERT: Well me walking through it ain't gonna stop it! I think she's trying to get rid of me.

NORA: Well I'll have you if Mary's finished with you Bert. I've forgotten what a bit of the other's like!

ROSIE (*looking at* PETER): Mum . . .!

NORA: How about you, Annie? D'you want him after me?

ANNIE: If there's anything left!

PETER: You're right dirty you lot!

BERT: I'll tell you, Pete, these women's worse than the men. And just you remember, Annie Crawley, there's many a good tune played on an old fiddle.

MARY: Hark at him. Your strings broke a long time ago. I'm only keeping you on to put the coal on the fire!

NORA: Poor old soul . . .

BERT: Oh, yer . . . Well I suppose I better be on me rounds. Where did I put my gas mask . . .

MARY: I thought you still had it on, love!

They all laugh.

ANNIE: Oh, Gawd . . . Who'd ever believe there was bombs dropping all around us . . .

MARY: Thank Christ we can laugh.

NORA: If you didn't . . .

BERT: Right then. I'm off.

MARY (*gives him a kiss on the cheek*): You be careful, love.

BERT: Don't worry.

ANNIE: See you later, Bert. Take care.

NORA: Tat ta, Bert. Watch yourself.

BERT: Will do. God bless yer. See you in the morning . . . (Leaving.) Underneath the arches, I dream my dreams away . . . (*He goes off.*)

MARY (*watching him leave*): Ah, he's not a bad old stick. Lucky to have him I suppose. He was badly wounded in the first world war. I mean, it's just luck, ain't it?

ANNIE (*pause*): Just luck.

NORA (*reflective*): yer, luck. (*She looks at* ANNIE.) Our men'll come back, Annie. Don't you worry yourself.

ANNIE: Yer. You can only hope, can't yer? And pray. What else can you do?

NORA: How about a game of cards?

MARY: A good idea. Come on, Annie, nothing like a gamble to help you forget . . .

ANNIE: All right, then . . . And Peter, you leave that bloody wireless alone if it don't work. Or you'll be electricuting yourself . . .

The three WOMEN *form into a group. They begin to play cards.* PETER, *with a long lead on the wireless, joins* ROSIE.

ROSIE: Don't it work yet?

PETER: Don't know what's up with it . . . Might be one of the valves gone.

ROSIE: It's right boring in here, ain't it?

PETER: Yer. But I'm glad the air-raid warning went before we went to bed. Me mum don't even give you a chance to get dressed if it goes in the middle of the night. She says: get dressed in the shelter.

ROSIE: My mum's the same. When I say I ain't dressed yet, she says: who wants to look at you?

PETER (*pause*): Yer.

ROSIE (*pause*): Did you go to school today?

PETER (*quietly, looking round*): No. Ain't been all the week.

ROSIE: The school-board man'll be round to your mum. The other day he came round to me mum and she went off alarming. She says at least when I'm in school, she knows where I am.

PETER: As long as they know where you are it's all right.

ROSIE: Yer. (*Pause.*) I see you the other Saturday.

PETER: Yer? Where?

ROSIE: Saturday morning pictures.

PETER: Oh, yer.

ROSIE (*pause*): With Sheila Clancy.

PETER (*pause*): If you get just there, (*He points.*) me mum can't see me and I'll get the back off . . . I've got me screw-driver down me shirt. Go on . . .

ROSIE (*moves*): She'll kill you if she sees you . . .

PETER: She's scared of electricity. I ain't.

ROSIE: I don't like things I can't see.

PETER *looks at the light bulb. Pause.*

You going Saturday morning pictures this week?

PETER: No. Going to sell fire-wood. Down the gap. Only didn't do it that other Saturday cause it was raining. Besides me and my mate knows where there's a load of tarry-blocks. This school got bombed and all the floor was wood. Right good for burning they are.

ROSIE: D'you know my friend who's older than me?

PETER: *Her.*

ROSIE: She got this lipstick, see. Said she could get me some. And stockings.

PETER: What for?

ROSIE: Film stars wear lipstick and stockings.

PETER: They don't get 'em from the sailors.

ROSIE: My friend's sixteen! She goes to work! And she ain't like everyone says she is. She told me. Besides, they're on our side, ain't they?

PETER: I don't care what she told you. What do I care?

ROSIE (*pause*): I thought you might . . . care. That's all. She has all these boys whistling her.

PETER: I don't whistle her!

ROSIE (*pause*): You can't whistle.

Pause. PETER laughs. ROSIE laughs.

NORA (*looks round*): Not too much laughing, Rosie. It's bound to lead to tears. (*She continues playing.*)

PETER (*quietly*): Always interfering, ain't they?

ROSIE: Yer. (*Pause.*) Have you nearly fixed that?

PETER (*looking*): It ain't the valves . . . They're all lit. Look!

ROSIE (*does so*): Oh, yer.

PETER *screws the back on. Pause.*

You had a fight the other day, didn't you?

PETER: I might have done.

Pause.

ROSIE: Someone told me.

PETER: Maybe they did. So?

ROSIE: Fancy fighting over a black girl . . . smelly things. She was that half-caste girl who lives with all them blacks near Watney Street, wasn't she? They're no good, blacks. That's what they say.

Pause. PETER gets up with the wireless and moves back to the top bunk.
ROSIE, as though she didn't care, moves towards the three women.

ANNIE: All right, Rosie?

ROSIE: Yer. Can't get the wireless working yet. It ain't the valves. They're all lit. . . We looked in the back . . .

ANNIE: Peter! I've told you! How many more times?

MARY: Ah, he don't mean any harm. We gonna have any wood this Saturday, Pete? I'm running short.

PETER: Yer. And tarry-blocks. Two for threepence.

MARY: Another one making money out of the bombing.

NORA: I'll have some, Peter. Don't forget Rosie's mum.

ANNIE: He better not forget his own mum — Up! Four kings and seven eight nine.

MARY: That's four games you've won, Annie. Your luck's in tonight. Come on, then, one more game and I think it'll be time for a cuppa.

PETER (*holding the wireless up*): It's coming through! (*Crackles.*) Nearly . . .

ROSIE: I'm tired. I wanna go to sleep.

NORA: Well close your eyes and sleep yer silly cow. Your bunk's over there.

ROSIE: I can't sleep with the wireless . . .

NORA: If you can sleep with that lot out there, you'll sleep through anything. Now shut up and let me concentrate . . .

PETER *turns up the wireless.*

RADIO: . . . 'Under the title, "Japan wants the Earth", the third episode of this series on Monday deals with the years between 1931 and 1939 when the Japanese went ahead with their "Divine Mission in Asia" under the cloak of an effective smoke-screen of propaganda. Efficiency, violence, and hypocrisy were the Japanese weapons, and China was the victim . . . Arthur Lucan and Kitty McShane bring Old Mother Riley back to the microphone on Saturday for the first of a new series of their popular shows. This week they will have Tommy Handley with them as guest star . . .'

The wireless crackles. PETER fiddles with it.

ROSIE *whispers in her mother's ear.*

NORA: D'you hear that, Annie? Your boy's got a black girl in tow.

ANNIE: He's got what?

NORA: Tell her, Rose . . .

ROSIE: Your Peter likes a black girl.

ANNIE: Peter . . . ? What you up to . . . ?

PETER (*angry*): These boys were throwing bricks at her! And some girls! Only her, on her own! D'you hear! I clumped 'em!

ANNIE (*pause*): All right, son . . . all right . . . That explains that cut on your face. I only need one . . .

MARY: Kids are bastards at times . . . That's it! Rummy! Sorry, Annie.

NORA: I only needed one card . . .

ANNIE: I wanted two. Oh, that's one of my favourites . . . Turn it up, Pete . .

Issy Bon sings 'My Mother's Eyes' on the wireless. All the women join in. ANNIE starts dancing with NORA, MARY with ROSIE. PETER sits and smiles.

BILLY DOD *enters, removing his hat. He waits until the song finishes before he makes his presence known.*

BILLY: What's this, eh? A party?

ANNIE: Christ, look what the wind's blown in.

NORA: Blimey! It's Jack Warner's side-kick: Jack Shit!

BILLY: Very funny. Well, you all seem in good spirits.

MARY: You've got a nose like a bleedin' bloodhound. We was just going to have a cup of tea.

BILLY: That's a bit of luck. Fancy a cuppa . . . Rough old night out there. The Royal Group of Docks is taking a right hiding. Coventry's taking a hammering as well. The Cathedral's been flattened by all accounts. (*He makes himself comfortable on a bunk.*) Densely populated area is Coventry. A lot of casualties . . .

ANNIE (*pause*): Christ . . . Turn the radio down a bit, son . . . (*She sits.*)

MARY (*pouring BILLY a tea from the flask*): Didn't see my old man on your travels, did you?

BILLY: Bert?

MARY: And the dog.

BILLY: Yer. We had a chin-wag just by Shadwell Park. I think he might have had a pint or two, like. Dog was very frisky . . .

MARY (*mocking*): Who, my Bert? While he's on duty? Never.

BILLY: You're having me on . . . Come off it Mary . . . Nice cuppa . . .

MARY: You don't think he'd be walking out there on a night like this without a few pints under his belt do yer? Not so likely. He still jumps in his sleep listening to the shells and bullets of the last soddin' war.

NORA: So who's been getting in trouble, Billy? Your mother'd turn in her grave if she could see you in that uniform.

BILLY: What's that supposed to mean? Listen . . . 'ere, Nora, times have changed. She'd be right proud I'd say.

ANNIE: 'Course she would.

BILLY: I've just looked in down Crane Wharf in Wapping. You heard about last night, I suppose.

ANNIE: Yer. Sissy Collins was telling me this morning.

MARY: What? Annie, you ain't very generous with the gossip . . .

BILLY: The warehouse next door caught a packet. So the women and children formed a chain, 'cause they was the only access to the river and fought the fire themselves. Caught it in time as well. Well most of the fire brigade was in West India Docks and round the Island.

ANNIE: Funny bleedin' set of priorities in this war lark . . . Like to know what would have happened if it had been Crane Wharf that had got hit. Who'd have taken water to all those women and children, eh?

BILLY: Have to protect the water-front, Annie. Vital for supplies.

ANNIE (*angry*): Nothing's so vital as human life!

Pause.

MARY: Any more gossip, then, Bill? Who you nicked lately?

BILLY: Not me if I can help it.

NORA: Don't give us all that. You nicked Harry Long last Friday.

BILLY: I didn't have any bloody option. The chief was with me. Caught him red-handed. Opening up the bleedin' chemist shop with a tin opener. Who's heard the likes of it . . . ?

ANNIE: That's a shame. I suppose if the chief wasn't with you, you'd have taken a back-hander.

BILLY: Leave it out girl! In front of these youngsters. What will they think of the law. Mustn't joke about things

like that. Right, Peter? Rosie? Still,
you're all nice and comfortable here.
Very nice too . . .

They are unconcerned.

ANNIE: You think we're safe do you,
Billy?

BILLY: Very tough these brick shelters.
More space than those Anderson ones.
Mind you, they had to be put up a bit
lively. Still tough, though.

ANNIE: That's true: they keep the rain
off . . .

BILLY: Plus you've got the flats one side
and the biscuit factory the other. Very
snug. Them Luffwaffe'd have to go
some to land one on here. Snug as a
bug in a rug . . . Nice cuppa . . .

MARY: Here, next time you drop in,
bring your bleedin' rations with you.
Everyone else does.

NORA: Yes. Copper or no copper, you
ought to pay your way. There's sugar
in that tea.

BILLY: I noticed. (*Slight pause.*) Your
brother still docking is he? Not been
called up? Still unloading the boats . . .

NORA: No he ain't. (*She pours him more
tea.*) And stop asking questions and
don't look a gift-horse in the face.

BILLY: I ain't working now, girl. What
your brother puts in his pocket's no
concern of mine.

MARY: Coppers never *stop* working.

BILLY: Don't you women trust anyone?

ANNIE: After what bleedin' Chamberlain
told us? Not so likely. D'you know,
there was preparation for evacuating
the women and kids as far back as
1931. But nobody told *us*. I bet no
one told the German women and
children either. This ain't a very
trusting world, Bill, if you ask me.

BILLY: I didn't know that. But I don't
see what good it would have done.
Just means a longer panic.

ANNIE: Balls. We've a right to know.

We're the people who have to fight it.
Suddenly there's a war. But no so
suddenly, eh?

BILLY: There's been wars all through
history. Don't know why they should
stop now. Do you?

ANNIE: Yes! Yes, I bloody well do!
(*She walks over to* PETER.) Him for
one. And my two girls. And my
husband. That's four reasons. D'you
want any more?

BILLY: No need to get emotional,
Annie. I didn't start the war did I?
Nothing to do with me. I don't like
it no more than you.

ANNIE: That's what I mean. Nobody
like its. Yet they still bloody
happen. Makes me sick.

MARY: Don't upset yourself, girl. Ain't
worth it.

NORA: I'll tell you what it is: it's men's
nature. They're violent. Afraid of
themselves. That's what makes them
violent: Fear.

MARY: My Bert ain't violent, Nora. All
men ain't violent. My Bert's as gentle
as a lamb. And I'll tell you another
thing: a bit of the other takes the
violence out of a man. Works like
a charm every time. That or the
allotment!

NORA: He's a rare one, that's all I can
say. But I'll keep that in mind . . .

BILLY (*rises*): It's all very enlightening,
girls, but duty calls. Must be about me
business. Lovely cuppa. Well then, I'll
be off. Shouldn't last much longer.

ANNIE: The war or the air-raid?

BILLY: The air-raid. Don't know about
the war. Rumour has it that Hitler's
planning an invasion. Be that as it
may, I've still got to apprehend the
criminals. I'll say goodnight to you . . .
(*He looks at his watch.*) Or is it good
morning . . . Quarter after mid-night.
Tat ta, ladies. On me way to Bethnal
Green tube station. The place is full.

On the stairs, everywhere. Ideal spot for the pick-pockets. Some crooks ain't got a bit of respect for conditions. D'you know, it's rumoured that little teams create a panic just to make the takings easier? Wouldn't believe it, would you?

ANNIE: I would.

BILLY: Yes . . . Right. I'm off. Thanks for the hospitality and I'll see you . . . (*Leaving.*)

MARY: All right, Nora, bring out the corn-beef and the gin —

BILLY (*stops*): Do . . .?

MARY (*laughs*): Falls for it every time . . .

BILLY: I don't think it's funny . . . (*He leaves.*)

PETER: Mum, Vera Lynn's on the wireless.

ANNIE: Turn it up, son. Let's have a good cry . . . (*She laughs.*)

Vera Lynn singing 'When the Lights Go On Again All Over the World.' The WOMEN *make up their beds. They sing intermittently to the wireless. An announcer comes on.* PETER *turns down the volume.*

MARY: Annie, is your youngest still wetting the bed down there? Lot of the kids are wetting the bed.

ANNIE: She's been all right these last couple of months. I didn't know what to say to the poor woman. I mean, my girl's never wet the bed before. She was ever so nice about it. Said she understood it perfectly. I didn't. You don't bring your kids up like that do you? Then she told me about the . . . 'enuresis allowance' and I wasn't to worry.

MARY: What's that for gawd's sake?

ANNIE: Well for soiling the beds. A sort of compensation.

NORA: D'you know, when I was first married, my old man used to get up

in his sleep and piss in my shoes. And in the cupboard. Wish I'd have known about that allowance. Could have claimed a fortune!

ANNIE: You silly cow! Not for those reasons. It's fer kids. Because they're afraid.

MARY: The day St Mary's and Michael's school got bombed I done more than wet me knickers!

They all laugh.

ANNIE: That was a miracle. Had it happened on Friday . . . God forbid.

MARY: I heard it. Just down Watney Street, I was. The whineing in the sky, then nothing. Then bang, like a paper bag slapped hard. I froze. Couldn't move. I said to myself: who'll be missing tomorrow? What children have stopped growing?

NORA (*pause*): Rosie, love, come on, get into the blankets and I'll tuck you in . . .

ROSIE: I ain't tired yet.

NORA: You will be in the morning. Come on . . .

ROSIE (*climbs into a bunk*): I'm hungry.

NORA: So am I. We're all hungry. Now get some sleep. (*She tucks her in.*)

ANNIE: Pete, you going to stay in the top bunk?

PETER: Yer.

ANNIE: Well, you can un-plug that wireless. You warm enough?

PETER *nods.*

ANNIE: Shall I read you a story?

PETER: Who, me?

ROSIE (*picks up*): D'you read Peter stories?

ANNIE: Yes.

ROSIE: Cor.

PETER (*embarrassed*): I'm going to un-plug the wireless . . . (*He does so.*) Then I'm going to sleep.

ANNIE: I'll read myself a story then . . .
You turning in, Mary, Nora?

MARY: All ready . . .

NORA: And me . . .

All the WOMEN *get into their bunks.
After they are all comfortable:*

ANNIE: I wonder what my old man's
doing at this moment . . .

MARY: Where is he?

ANNIE: In Italy.

MARY: Probably a big Italian woman.

ANNIE: I wouldn't be surprised.

MARY: I'm only joking, love.

ANNIE: Seems . . . unimportant. The war
makes it unimportant. You only pray
that they . . . live, don't you, don't
you. A bit of the other don't make
a lot of sense these days.

PETER (*annoyed*): Mum!

NORA: He's off again. He's definitely
heading for a white collar.

ANNIE: You can't say nothing about his
father. He thinks he's fighting the war
alone. Ha. (*Pause.*) He sent him home
a toy boat, with love. And a piece of
rock from a volcano.

NORA: It's a good boy respects his
father. Goes a long way to respecting
yourself. Right, Pete, son?

PETER: Yer. All right.

MARY: You know I do like that tune
what Zoë Gail sings . . .
I'm going to get lit up
When the lights go on in London.
I'm going to get lit up
As I've never been before.
You will find me on the tiles.
You will find me wreathed in smiles.
I'm going to get lit up.
I'll be visible for miles . . .'

ANNIE: And how about Vera Lynn
singing: 'the little boy who Santa
Claus forgot . . .' Makes me cry that
does. Don't make my Pete none too
happy . . .

NORA: Annie, laughing makes *you* cry.
Right watery brain you've got. Soft as
putty you silly cow . . . You'll get
harder as you get older. You'll see.

ANNIE: Yes. It's probably for the best.

MARY (*pause*): D'you hear what they're
saying about the Local Defence
Volunteers? Makes my Bert turn blue.

ANNIE: What?

MARY: The initials — LDV. Look, duck
and vanish. Mind you, my old man
never did have a sense of humour.

Pause.

ANNIE: Goodnight, then . . .

MARY: Night, love.

NORA: Night all . . .

*Quietness. The sound of distant
bombing.*

BERT (*staggers in holding the dog strap,
covered in dust*: Mary! Mary!

MARY (*from the bunk*): Bert?

BERT: Mary!

MARY (*gets out of the bunk*): What . . . ?

ANNIE *and* NORA *get out of their
bunks. Also* PETER.

BERT: Mary!

MARY (*pause*): What is it, love? Look
at you . . .

BERT (*pause, holds up the dog lead*):
Mary . . .

MARY: Oh, God . . .

PETER *breaks down, turns to his
bunk.*

ACT TWO

PETER *is alone in the shelter. He is reading a book by candle-light, sitting on the mattresses.*

ROSIE (*off*): Pete!

PETER *hides the book.*
ROSIE *enters.*

Your mum said you might be in here. (*Pause.*) What you doing? It's sunny outside.

PETER: Doing nothing.

ROSIE: Just sitting here on your own?

PETER: It's all right, en it? What you want?

ROSIE: I've got two fags. My friend gave 'em to me. American ones. Want one?

PETER: Don't mind . . .

ROSIE: Here y'are.

They smoke uncomfortably.

PETER: Smell don't they? (*Pause.*) Once slept on these mattresses. I lifted up me pillow and there was a rat underneath. I put the pillow back and slept on it all night. Might have been dreaming . . . That's what me mum said. Wasn't there in the morning . . .

ROSIE (*moves*): I can't smell . . . Not properly. Smell the shutes, sometimes . . .

PETER: Me dad says American fags are made out of camel shit.

ROSIE (*puts her cigarette out*): Turned me right off, you have.

PETER: He smokes Nutbrown. Don't half stink.

ROSIE: What you doing in here?

PETER: I told you. Nothing.

ROSIE: Just sitting?

PETER: Yer.

ROSIE: When it's all sunny?

PETER: So what?

ROSIE: Just silly that's all.

PETER (*pause*): Wha' d'you want, anyway.

ROSIE: Me mum's gone to a funeral.

PETER: Oh.

ROSIE: Think that's what she said . . . Don't know why she goes. Makes her cry.

PETER: My mum's the same.

ROSIE (*pause*): Wasn't it a shame about Blackie?

PETER *shrugs it off.*
Pause.

Don't you think so?

PETER: This fag smells like camel shit.

ROSIE: You don't have to smoke it if you don't want to.

PETER (*pause*): What d'you want, anyway? If you like the sun so much, what you doing here?

ROSIE: Will you be glad when we go down hopping?

PETER: Yer.

ROSIE: So will I. It's good en it?

PETER: Yer. Not picking though. Not in the mornings when all the hops is wet.

ROSIE: No. That's horrible. Cuts your legs and arms to pieces, all them bines. Where I fell over last year carrying the bin, I've still got a scar. Look! (*She lifts her skirts.*) See?

PETER (*looks and turns away*): I don't want to see your stupid scar.

ROSIE: Just showing you, that's all. (*She leaves her skirt up.*) Nothing else . . .

PETER (*pause*): You better go then. Won't be sunny much longer.

ROSIE (*pause*): I had an egg this morning.

PETER: So what?

ROSIE: My uncle who works in the docks fetched six round to me mum.

PETER: I don't like eggs.

ROSIE (*pause*): D'you like me?

PETER: You tell tales.

ROSIE: About that black girl?

PETER: Yer. And about the wireless.

ROSIE (*pause*): Sorry. Honest.

PETER: Ah, it's all right. Don't worry me.

ROSIE: Why did you have a fight? D'you like her?

PETER: Don't even know her.

ROSIE: Why then? She's a blackie.

PETER: D'you know her?

ROSIE: No. I don't know blackies. Me mum, no, me dad wouldn't let me know 'em.

PETER: Well then . . .

ROSIE (*pause*): Well what then?

PETER: Nothing.

ROSIE: Besides, down the other end of Cable Street the black men live on white women. Me dad was telling me mum. They're called ponces. Something like that.

PETER: That's up the end of Cable Street.

ROSIE: Black people's black.

PETER: So are white people.

ROSIE: White people are different.

PETER: How about Hitler killing all the Jews and other people. He's white.

ROSIE: Oh, I don't care. Except they smell.

PETER: D'you go around sniffing people then?

ROSIE (*laughs*): Don't be mad . . . (*She can see the book.*) Is that a book?

PETER: So what?

A long pause.

ROSIE: Must be getting dark out by now.

PETER (*fed up*): Yer . . .

ROSIE (*sighs, pause*): Wish I was sixteen. Like my friend. (*Pause.*) But you don't have to be sixteen to do what she does . . . Anyone can kiss, can't they?

PETER: Who wants to?

ROSIE: It's easy en it?

PETER: So what?

ROSIE: Remember when you kissed me that time; when we was playing kiss-chase? We was behind the door leading out to the yard. (*Pause.*) Remember what else you done?

PETER: No.

ROSIE: I do.

PETER: So what?

ROSIE: Fancy me mum saying you was going to be a priest. After you done that . . .

PETER: Your mum's a silly old cow.

ROSIE: I didn't tell her though.

PETER: Ta.

ROSIE (*pause*): D'you want to do it again?

PETER (*takes his book out*): I want to read me book.

ROSIE: I know how to kiss properly now. My friend told me.

PETER: What?

ROSIE: I'll show you?

PETER: Kissing's kissing. What's there to show?

ROSIE: Shall I?

PETER: I know.

ROSIE: Look . . . (*She kisses him.*)

PETER (*reels back*): What you doing? You put your tongue in my mouth.

ROSIE: Called a French kiss. (*A long pause. She moves slowly towards him. She kisses him again.*) See?

PETER (*pause*): Yer.

He moves towards her, kisses her. He becomes more passionate. He puts his hand on her breast. ROSIE *takes his hand and puts it under her shirt. The siren begins, quiet and then loud.*

ROSIE: The warning! (*She gets up.*) Me mum'll kill me if I ain't upstairs! (*She runs out.*) She'll be back by now!

PETER *watching her leave. The siren is very loud. He masturbates in his pocket. The siren stops. He stops.*

ANNIE (*entering quickly. She carries his gas mask*): Why didn't you come and get your gas mask? Didn't you hear the siren? (*Pause.*) What's the matter?

PETER: Nothing. I was reading me book.

ANNIE: Why ain't the lights come on? Are you all right? Sick or something? You must be sickening for something . . .

PETER: You can't even see me. (*The lights come on.*) Can you . . .

ANNIE: Something's wrong with you. Don't have to see to know . . . Here, take this . . . (*She passes him the gas mask.*) I was just sewing your trousers up. Bleeding arse hanging out of 'em. Keep out of the bombed houses in the future. You know clothes are on ration. Times I tell you.

NORA (*enters*): Hello, Annie, I've never seen this one run so quickly . . .

ROSIE: It's still light . . .

ANNIE: Hello, love. I suppose it caught you with your drawers down as well.

NORA: Can't even wait 'til it's dark these days. Mary not here?

MARY: Just arrived . . . Bert's with me . . .

BERT: I thought it was very nice of her to invite me. You notice I'm the pack-mule as usual? You'll be happy to know, ladies, I ain't on duty till nine.

ANNIE: That's nice to know, Bert.

MARY: A pillar of strength.

NORA (*sings*): And so say all of us!

ALL (*sing*):
And so say all of us!
Until he's let into the cellar,
For he's a jolly good Fella!
And so say all of us!

BERT: Thank you ladies. You got the wireless, Pete?

PETER (*looks at his mother*): I'll go'n get it . . .!

ANNIE: Oh, all right. Be quick. If you hear a plane, leave it!

PETER *runs off.*

This is good. Ain't brought a thing with me. Except my boy's bleedin' trousers and needle and cotton.

MARY: Well we ain't had daylight raids for a while.

BERT: Reason for that, don't worry.

MARY: All right, clever clogs. What's the reason?

NORA: See better, surely . . .

BERT: Not at all. There'll be no invasion now. Don't you worry yourself about that.

ANNIE: Ain't we worth it then, our little island?

BERT: The silly bugger's marched against Uncle Joe. Thousands and thousands of troops going into Russia. I'll tell you what. He's bitten off more than he can chew. Bleedin' right laugh now. Kissing Uncle Joe: as red as they are. That's our Mr Churchill . . .

MARY: Ain't stopped 'em bombing us out of house and home.

BERT: How many more times, Mary. You don't listen; I told you. Workers keep a country going. Hitler ain't interested in military installations, seeing as how he ain't coming. He wants us. He'll bring the country to its knees if he destroys us. Us I mean; living shoulder to shoulder in our tiny streets and houses and buildings. All he's got to do is make a bee-line for the Thames. Bob's your uncle.

Labour: the back-bone of any system . . .

ANNIE: Ain't there any rules at all in this bleedin' war? Bombing women and children ain't war. It's murder.

NORA: You know what they say about rules, Annie. They're made to be broken.

ANNIE: Pity men don't have babies. Wouldn't be so quick to kill if they suffered like us to give life. Very fond of taking it away . . .

BERT *(making himself comfortable)*: Human beings is more savage than any animal, I'll grant you that . . .

MARY: Now don't start getting morbid, Bert. You promised you would forget. She's gone. There's no use in resurrecting the dead.

BERT: She was useful. Not just as a pet. Why, she could pick up the sounds of enemy planes long before we could. Sharp ears she had . . . Brave as they make 'em . . .

ROSIE: Will you get another dog, Mr Walker? One the same?

BERT: No, Rosie, can't afford to feed 'em, apart from anything else. Maybe when it's all over . . . *(Pause.)* Listen. They've started.

ANNIE *looks towards the entrance. Quiet. Distant sound of explosions.*

PETER *(comes back)*: I'm here, mum.

ANNIE *(nods her head)*: Better finish these trousers . . . *(She sews.)*.

PETER *(gets on the top bunk and plugs in)*: *D*on't say it, mum . . .

ANNIE: So long as you know . . .

BERT: How about a poem?

MARY: Choice! You stand there saying poems and I'll go and fetch something to drink! With that lot . . .

BERT: I'll *read* a poem, then *I'll* go. Fair enough? Right It's called 'The Soldier'.

NORA: Bit of hush please for Bert's poem reading. Go on Bert.

ROSIE: What's a poem?

BERT: What's a poem? Blimey, I know your schooling's been interrupted but that's the latest. Right then. Here goes:

The Soldier

If I should die, think only this of me:
That there's some corner of a foreign field
That is forever England. There shall be
In that rich earth a richer dust concealed;
A dust whom England bore, shaped made aware,
Gave, once, her flowers to love, her ways to roam,
A body of England's, breathing English air,
Washed by the rivers, blest by suns of home.

And think this heart, all evil shed away,
A pulse in the eternal mind, no less,
Gives somewhere back the thoughts by England given;
Her sights and sounds; dream happy as her day;
And laughter, learnt of friends; and gentleness,
In hearts of peace, under an English heaven.

They all clap.

MARY: He thinks he wrote that for him.

BERT: We was in the same regiment. Poor sod went and got sick and died. I don't know how he wrote that . . . We was up to our ear-holes in mud most of the time. Ha! The Great War . . . All of them men . . .

ANNIE: That was lovely, Bert. But I didn't like it.

BERT: Bit arse about face, Annie.

ANNIE: Soldiers being sung about ain't right. You might as well sing about those bastards dropping bombs down on us. It'd be the same. Wouldn't it?

MARY (*pause*): All right then, Bert, love. You go'n make us a nice pot of tea.

BERT (*pause*): Yer. (*He puts the book in his pocket.*) Yer . . . (*Leaving.*)

PETER (*as BERT passes*): I liked it Mr Walker.

BERT *touches him.*

MARY: Love, pick me knitting up for me. It's on the dresser.

BERT (*leaves*): Yer . . .

NORA: I think you've upset him, Annie.

ANNIE: Well . . .

MARY: It's 'cause he was in the same regiment.

ANNIE: It's . . . just me. I'll give him a big kiss when he comes in . . .

NORA, *sitting on a bunk, wipes her eyes.*

ROSIE: Mum . . . ?

NORA: Be quiet.

ANNIE: Something wrong, Nora? What's up, love?

NORA (*pause*): I'll be all right . . .

ROSIE: Me mum's been to a funeral.

NORA: Who told you that?

ROSIE: You put your black scarf on . . . I thought . . .

NORA: Got funerals on the mind.

MARY: Not like you, Nora, shedding a tear.

NORA (*blows her nose*): I had an horrible shock today. About ten this morning there's this knock on the door. And there's this bloke standing there. Blimey, if it ain't my Dennis's mate who's off the same boat. Well he came round once, not so long ago, when their boat pulled into London, or somewhere. Well anyway, he was from Liverpool. Did you know that my Dennis's on that destroyer called *Onslow* whose captain. Sherbrooke, I think his name was, got a medal —

MARY: Blimey, Nora, are you going to give us a history of the navy . . . ?

NORA: Listen, Mary, when a strange man — a sailor at that — knocks on your door, you know what people's like. Anyway, there he is, standing at the door. Seemed like yesterday he was just saying hello and was going off up to Liverpool to see his own family. And there he was, alone. (*Pause.*) His whole family . . . gone. A direct hit. Out like a flame. (*Pause.*) He said he didn't know what to do. He was lost. Like a little boy lost. I've never seen a man so empty. I said to him that my Dennis was back with the Russian convoys. I didn't know what to say to him. (*Pause.*) What can you say to a man alone?

ANNIE (*moved*): Nora, that's terrible. Terrible. (*She loses her temper.*) Terrible!

MARY: Now you've upset Annie. Come on, Annie, sit down, love.

ANNIE: Oh, God . . . Why?

MARY: You're asking the right person . . . 'Cause I don't bleedin' know!

BERT (*enters*): Something wrong . . .?

MARY: Nora's had a bit of an upset. Cup of tea'll cheer her up.

BERT: And a bit of music. Any luck there, young Pete?

PETER (*vague*): Oh, yer. It's coming.

BERT: Plenty of volume, son. It's raining a lot of iron out there. Looks like Woolwich Arsenal's copping it . . . Right. Tea. Where's the mugs.

ROSIE (*picks up cups scattered around*): Here they are, Mr Walker . . .

BERT: Good girl. (*He pours tea, hands it out.*)

MARY: Did you pick up my knitting?

BERT: Oh, Christ.

MARY: Got a memory like a sieve . . .

BERT: I'll have a cuppa first. Rosie, one for you . . . And one for Pete . . .

PETER: Can you hold it for me . . .

ROSIE: Have you got the station?

PETER: Think so . . .

ROSIE: I can hear it . . .

BERT: Turn it up, son . . .

WIRELESS: Wardens from Paddington and Glasgow will compete in ARP Knowledge in a radio contest on Saturday night. John Suagge puts the questions to the two teams and the match will be umpired by ARP officers from Coventry and Southampton.

MARY (*to* BERT): I thought your ears would cock up . . .

WIRELESS: This week marks the second anniversary of Dunkirk and on Friday a tribute will be paid to the little ships that did such gallant work in the evacuation of the BEF. In the story of 'The Pride of Britain', an imaginary pleasure steamer, you will hear the story of all the hundreds of small craft which helped to serve Britain in those black yet glorious days that ushered in June, 1940 . . . (*Fades, crackles.*)

ANNIE: Very glorious and I don't think . . .

BERT: Come off it, Annie. Dunkirk was the true spirit of England.

ANNIE: Nothing that happens in war is glorious to me, Bert. I'm sorry, love. Everytime I hear about all the heroics I think back to March this year. Got caught down in Wapping. Just been to see me father in St George's. The raid was sudden. Me and me sister decided to get home rather than take shelter. (*She nods at* PETER.) I was worried about him more than anything. Suddenly there's this terrible bang. One of those little houses in Garnet street was hit. The next thing, we see this woman standing in the street screaming. We run to her. She was

beside herself. All she kept saying was: my children, my children. We couldn't hold her. She ran into the debris of her house and we chased her. (*Pause.*) We found the children, Bert. The remains reminded me of dirty sacks and dog's meat. (*Pause.*) That's what heroics mean to me. For every hero there's a sufferer . . .

RADIO: . . . Tonight at 9.15 you can hear 'Woman at War', the weekly magazine programme for and by women in organised war jobs in all parts of the country. Factory workers, nurses, land army, women in the Civil Defence forces, NAAFI and canteen and hostel work, Ambulance and Transport Services, and many others take part along with WRNS, ATS and WAAF. Carroll Gibbons will provide the music in this popular programme and Hilde Marchant will answer questions raised by women in war jobs. (*Pause.*) The time is 8.30.

Music. Signature tune of Ambrose and his Orchestra.
NORA *puts her hand to her ear.*

ROSIE: What's a matter, mum?

NORA: Shsss . . .

ANNIE: What is it Nora? Turn that down, Pete.

Distant bombing is heard.

MARY: Blimey, Bert, that sounds near.

BERT: Wouldn't be surprised if it wasn't West India Docks. I'll, er, go'n get your knitting, Mary.

MARY: You'll do nothing of the sort!

BERT: Look, I've only got to cross the yard. What is it, ten feet and I'm in the block. Don't be silly. Besides, I've got to pick up me helmet and torch. I'm duty-bound. An air-raid's an air-raid.

MARY: All right, then. Well put something over your head.

BERT (*amused, puts his handkerchief over his head*): That should save me a headache from flying schrapnel . . .

PETER *laughs.*

ANNIE: He's tormenting you, Mary.

MARY: I'll give him torment. Peter, you turn that wireless up. What I can't hear I can't worry about. And you be quick . . . I want to get on with me knitting.

Music louder. Anne Shelton singing 'It Can't Be Wrong'.

BERT: Well give us the pot then and I'll make a fresh cuppa.

NORA: Bert, make it in my flat. I've left the door open. Got fuck all to nick, I should worry.

BERT: Your turn next. Besides, I want to change me socks. Hate to have an accident with dirty socks on. Won't be long. (*He leaves.*)

ROSIE: Mum, I want to go to the lav.

NORA: Well want on.

ROSIE: I do!

NORA: Well just step out in the yard.

ROSIE: Not that . . .

NORA: Listen here my girl. You just be quick. When you come down bring the blankets down. Put 'em on your head. Be quick.

ROSIE *leaves.*

ANNIE: None of us have got a bleedin' thing with us.

MARY: Well it was almost daylight when the raid started. Don't usually last long.

NORA: This one seems to be going on forever. (*Pause.*) My Rosie's a long time . . .

ANNIE: Give over, Nora. She's just walked out the bleedin' door.

NORA (*pause*): I can't remember whether I pulled the black-out down . . . She'll have to turn on the light . . .

MARY: She'll remember.

NORA: She'll be more interested in getting her bum down. Did I draw 'em or not . . . ? You forget don't you . . . ?

ANNIE: You ain't going to rest until you know, are you?

NORA: Bloody nuisance she is. Wants to go in the most awkward moments. I'll go'n make sure . . . (*She leaves.*)

ANNIE: After what she heard, I don't blame her . . .

MARY: That's what being a mother is, Annie. Spend the rest of your life worrying about your kids. Romance don't last long does it?

ANNIE: That's a fact.

MARY: Bit of an handicap. I don't mind telling you. Six kids I've brought up. Gawd knows how we survived. Especially during the twenties. And he was away before that in the Great War. Then the depression.

ANNIE: Now this.

MARY: Makes you wonder what life's all about don't it. Short on romance, short on money, short on work, short on anything resembling security. What a bleedin' life.

ANNIE: Only thing us women ain't short of is pain killers and sanitary towels.

MARY: Well, mustn't hold up the war effort because of period pains. Which, thank gawd, ain't a problem of mine anymore.

ANNIE: We're soon old, Mary, ain't we?

PETER (*turns the wireless down*): Mum.

ANNIE: What?

PETER: Why are there wars?

ANNIE (*pause*): I don't know, son. I honestly don't know.

MARY: My Bert says it's to do with economics.

ANNIE: That's just a bleedin' word to

me. War means killing. It's something about *men,* Mary. Something in 'em. Something . . . spiteful. They take pleasure in the pain of it all.

MARY: Well, Hitler's a bloody lunatic that's for sure. Greedy bastard, if nothing else.

ANNIE: Takes more than one man to make war. It's not that though . . . it's something else.

PETER: What something else?

ANNIE: I don't know!

PETER: Christ . . .

ANNIE: One day you'll be a man. Ask yourself the question then.

MARY: Well whatever it is Annie, working people like us gain sod all out of it. The 'better world' we're fighting for ain't going to fall in our laps. I've learnt that much from the last bleedin' turn-out.

ANNIE: All I do know, that in times like these, people seem a bit nearer to God. It's mad. When we're all faced with the prospect of dying, we draw closer to one another. I can believe that somewhere in Germany, another woman is saying exactly what I'm saying. But the bloody madness of it all is, that in any event, we're all going to die, sooner or later. Why don't we act in the same way? Do we have to have war to prove that we're all human after all? I mean, where will it end? Now there's talk of these rockets that can travel seventy miles! Where will it end?

MARY: Where all life ends, love. Six feet under. The most you can hope for these days is a comfortable journey.

ROSIE (*enters*): Me mum's making sandwiches . . . (*She puts some blankets down.*)

MARY: Bless her.

ANNIE: I'm feeling a bit hungry myself. Did she have bread?

ROSIE: Yer. I lined up for it this morning: all morning!

ANNIE: Better than going hungry, Rosie . . .

MARY: I've got a loaf for later. Bert managed to dodge the queue by pretending to inspect the black-out precautions. Crafty sod. I don't blame him though. He did enough queuing in the trenches.

BERT (*enters with tea. He wears his helmet. He has a bag with knitting in*): Here you are, love. I didn't forget this time. What's up with the radio, Pete.

PETER: They was talking . . . (*He turns it up.*)

WIRELESS: Ambrose playing 'I Don't Want to Set the World on Fire', sung by Anne Shelton.

BERT *sings the song and pours tea.*

NORA (*enters with a bag and blankets*): I fetched your blankets, Annie. Your door was wide open. I pulled it to . . .

ANNIE: I left in a bit of a hurry! Didn't leave me knickers on the stairs did I? Wouldn't be the first time . . .

PETER *laughs.*

BERT: That made him laugh, Annie.

ANNIE: Takes the piss out of me. I just freeze when that bloody siren goes. Does something to me. Can't stand it. Don't matter what I'm doing, I just run. And drag him with me.

PETER: Pulls me out of bed she does. Won't even let me get dressed.

ANNIE: You can always get dressed. You can't have your bloody life back if a bomb explodes in your face. Just do what you're told!

BERT: Peter's a good lad. He's my mate. Misses the old dog, don't you son? I know. So do I.

MARY: Bert!

BERT: Sorry.

NORA: Come on. Get stuck in. There's jam on those, what I had from last year's fruit picking. Strawberrry.

PETER: Rosie, could you pass me a jam sandwich?

ROSIE (*does so*): Can I sit up there with you?

PETER (*moves over*): Come on . . .

ROSIE *sits next to him.*

MARY: Well the war's over between those two . . .

ANNIE: You're making him blush . . .

NORA: Look like a pair of love-birds up there —

The wireless suddenly goes very quiet. Heavy bombing is heard. Everyone remains still.

BERT: Jesus . . . (*To* MARY:) I've got to go, love. That sounds pretty close to me.

MARY (*pause*): You ain't ate your jam sandwich.

BERT: Put it in the bag. I'll have it when I come back.

(*He touches her.*) Don't worry, girl. I'll be all right. Say an Our Father and three Hail Mary's for me. All right?

MARY (*touches his face*): Silly sod . . .

BERT: Right, Pete, son. You're in charge. Keep tuned in. Nothing like a bit of music to sooth the nerves. (*He looks around.*) I don't know what we'd do without you. (*He leaves.*)

Heavy bombing is heard again.

MARY (*goes towards the entrance*): Bert . . . !

ANNIE: Mary . . . (*Consoles her.*) He'll be all right.

MARY: I didn't mind so much when he had the dog. A bit of company for him. I used to think to myself, well if he's got to . . . go, at least he won't be on his own.

NORA: He'll be back. Remember the song, Mary? Old soldiers never die: they only loose their balls!

The WOMEN *laugh. Another loud bang. They stop. Pause. Laugh again.*

ANNIE: Jesus Christ. What a state to be in. Don't know if to laugh or cry.

NORA: I wish I could go to sleep and wake up when it was all over.

Another loud bang. All still.

ANNIE (*moves towards* PETER): Sounds as though they're right over us.

MARY (*walks slightly towards the entrance*): God . . .

NORA (*pause*): My Dennis is on the high seas now. Freezing cold, you know, in them waters . . . Mary, love, come and sit down . . . Come away from the door . . .

Bombing.
A long pause. Quiet. PETER *turns the wireless up. Pause.*

WIRELESS: His Majesty's First Minister, the Prime Minister, the right honourable Mr Winston Churchill:

CHURCHILL: I have now served for two years exactly to a day as the King's First Minister. Therefore I thought it would be a good thing if I had a talk to you on the broadcast to look back a little on what we have come through, to consider how we stand now and to peer cautiously, but at the same time resolutely, into the future . . .

ANNIE: Turn that down a bit, son . . . I can just see him there, sitting with his crystal ball in front of him. You know, it makes me sick when I hear people talking about the future when we ain't got an inkling what's going on today.

MARY: Ain't it always the way, love . . . I don't need him telling me my future at my time of life. I know it right enough meself: tomorrow I'll be a day older. The days that follow'll probably bring sickness. And one bleedin' day me toes'll be curling up!

NORA: You ain't half cheerful, Mary . . .

ROSIE: What you always got to talk about dying for, mum?

MARY: Ah, young Rosie, how lovely to be young. And you're right, love. We shouldn't be talking about it.

ANNIE: It's the way people do talk about it that makes it so . . . frightening. It's like I'm saying. For instance, dying is an everyday occurrence but look at the way we all go about it. As though it was some form of ever bleedin' lasting torture. I mean, we can't even die with dignity. Round the grave there's people crying with broken hearts and sad memories. Flowers galore and posh black cars. Why, you'll never be given so many flowers during a soddin' lifetime, but when they do arrive, you're past looking! On the one day you stop, so everyone is giving and loving. That's what's bloody sick about dying. That's what's sick about life and living . . . Honour the dead and slaughter the living. That's how the picture looks to me.

MARY: Annie, everyone's afraid of dying. And it's hard to die with dignity when there's pain. Not only in yourself, but in those around you. The ones you leave.

NORA: Breaks my heart, those who are left behind.

ANNIE: I don't know . . . In a funny way, death's buried before it happens . . . sort of . . .

PETER: What's that mean, mum?

NORA: Yer, you've lost me there, Annie.

ANNIE: It just seems to me that natural . . . things go by the board most of the time. And unnatural things, like wars, well we allow those sort of things to occur. Instead of fighting disease, we fight each other. Instead of facing up to the fact that one day we must die, we live out our lives as though we were here forever. And so people become greedy and . . . selfish and violent. And so it goes on. My God, I hope it ain't too much to ask, that when I do die, or am dying, I'll be able to say quietly to myself: time to catch the midnight boat and I've enjoyed the trip so far. And those who I leave behind will enjoy tomorrow's sunshine. That ain't asking for too much, surely?

NORA: To leave a bit of sunshine is lovely. I really like that, Annie.

MARY: And your insurance paid up, Nora. Don't forget that!

They laugh.

PETER: It must be nearly finished now, mum. Shall I turn it up?

ANNIE: Might as well.

The wireless crackles. Churchill is still speaking.

CHURCHILL: If we look back today over the course of the war as it has so far unfolded, we can see that it seems to divide itself into four very clearly defined chapters. The first ended with the over-running by the Nazis of Western Europe and with the fall of France. The second chapter, Britain alone, ended with Hitler's attack upon Russia. I will call the third chapter which then began, 'the Russian glory'. May it long continue. The fourth chapter opened at Pearl Harbour, when the military party in Japan treacherously attacked the United States and Great Britain in the Far East. That is where we are now . . .

Therefore tonight I give you a message of good cheer. You deserve it, and the facts endorse it. But be it good cheer or be it bad cheer will make no difference to us; we shall drive on to the end, and do our duty, win or die. God helping us, we can do no other . . .

An enormous bang is heard. Falling masonry.

ANNIE: Holy Mother of God! What was that?

MARY: Listen . . .

NORA (*puts her arm round* ROSIE): Keep close, love.

ANNIE: I've never heard one that close before. Almost like it was next door. The factory, or the flats; It's quietening down now . . .

MARY: Yes . . .

PETER: It's all right, mum. We're safe in here —

The lights go out.

ANNIE: Oh, no!

Outside searchlights beat the sky. Distant bombing. BERT is on an emergency police phone.

BERT: I'm telling you to get round here! The bleeding shelter's got a factory on it! There's people in there! My missus is in there! (*Pause.*) I don't fucking care if they've sunk every ship this side of the English channel! My missus is buried alive in that shelter! It's completely covered! There be no air! No! You can't get a bulldozer to it. It's between the flats and the bloody factory! We've got to shift it with our bare hands! D'you hear! My missus is in there!

Back in the shelter.

PETER: It's all right, mum. I've got some matches in me pocket . . . (*He strikes one.*)

MARY: You got your candles handy, Annie; otherwise I'll get ours . . .

ANNIE: Yes. Hold it a sec. (*She brings out two candles.*)

PETER (*lights them*): Shall I light some for you Mrs Walker?

MARY: Hold on a minute, son . . . Ah, got him . . .

PETER *lights two more.*

NORA (*taking candles from her bag*): Here y'are, Pete; light these as well . . . Anyone would think it was Christmas . . .

The stage should be lit by candle light mostly.

ANNIE: What a bang. Whatever was it.

PETER: Some bombs weigh a thousand pounds.

MARY: I think that one was in tons.

NORA: Listen . . .

ANNIE: What is it, Nora?

NORA: It's gone very quiet.

ANNIE: Yes. Must be all over, eh?

MARY: I wouldn't be surprised.

ANNIE: Thank Gawd. Come on then 'All Clear'. Let's hear you.

MARY: My Bert should be back pretty soon now.

ANNIE: Suppose we better hang on till he comes. Just as well. (*Pause.*) I feel very tired . . .

NORA: It's been a bleedin' long night. Never mind, Rosie, you needn't go to school today. Thought that'd make you smile.

ANNIE: These youngsters love it . . . It's getting warm in here . . . They won't get a lot of work out of me today . . . Come on then, Bert . . .

MARY: You won't get him hurrying.

ANNIE: Always bloody waiting . . . Wait for the air-raid to begin. Wait for it to stop. I don't know . . .

The three WOMEN blow out the candles.

Royal Court Writers Series

Published to coincide with each production in the Royal Court
Theatre's main auditorium, this new series fulfils the dual
function of programme and playscript.

RSC Playtexts

Published to coincide with productions in the RSC's small theatres (The Other Place in Stratford-upon-Avon, the Gulbenkian Studio for the Company's annual visit to Newcastle upon Tyne, and The Pit in London), this new series fulfills the dual function of programme and playscript.

If you would like to receive, free of charge, regular information about new plays and theatre books from Methuen, please send your name and address to:

The Marketing Department (Drama)
Methuen London Ltd
North Way
Andover
Hampshire SP10 5BE